KEYBOARD ACCOMPANIMENT
GRADE 4

Scott Foresman

Editorial Offices: Parsippany, New Jersey • Glenview, Illinois • New York, New York
Sales Offices: Parsippany, New Jersey • Duluth, Georgia • Glenview, Illinois
Coppell, Texas • Ontario, California

ISBN: 0-382-34487-1

Copyright © 2002, Pearson Education, Inc.

All Rights Reserved. Printed in the United States of America. This publication is protected by Copyright and permission should be obtained from the publisher prior to any prohibited reproduction, storage in a retrieval system, or transmission in any form by any means, electronic, mechanical, photocopying, recording, or likewise. For information regarding permission(s), write to: Permissions Department, Scott Foresman, 1900 East Lake Avenue, Glenview, Illinois 60025.

3 4 5 6 7 8 9 10 V003 09 08 07 06 05 04 03 02

Credits and Acknowledgments

Cover Photography: Jade Albert for Scott Foresman.

Cover Design: Steven Curtis Design, Inc.

Electronic Production: Martini Graphic Services.

Acknowledgments

Credit and appreciation are due publishers and copyright owners for use of the following: 4: "Turn the Beat Around" from the Motion Picture *The Specialist*, Words and music by Peter Jackson, Jr. and Gerald Jackson. Copyright © 1975 by Unichappell Music Inc. This arangement Copyright © 2001 by Unichappell Music Inc. International Copyright Secured. All Rights Reserved. 10: "Put a Little Love in Your Heart" by Jimmy Holiday, Randy Myers and Jackie DeShannon. © 1969 (Renewed) EMI Unart Catalog Inc. All Rights Reserved. Used by Permission. WARNER BROS. PUBLICATIONS U.S. INC., Miami, FL 3014. 13: "Haul Away, Joe" © 2002 Pearson Education, Inc. 14: "Gakavik" (The Partridge) English words © 2002 Pearson Education, Inc. 15: "Tsuki" (The Moon) from *Children's Songs from Japan*. Florence White and Kazuo Akiyama. © 1960 Edward B. Marks Music Company. Copyright renewed. Used by permission. All rights reserved. 16: "Limbo Like Me" New words and new music adapted by Massie Patterson and Sammy Heyward. (Based on a traditional song) TRO–© 1963 (Renewed) Ludlow Music, Inc., New York, NY. Used by permission. 18: "Waitin' for the Light to Shine" from *Big River*. Words and music by Roger Miller. Copyright © 1985 Sony/ATV Songs LLC and Roger Miller music. This arrangement copyright © 2001 Sony/ATV Songs LLC and Roger Miller Music. All Rights Administered by Sony/ATV Music Publishing, 8 Music Square West, Nashville, TN 37203. International Copyright Secured. All Rights Reserved. Used by Permission. 20: "Sonando" by Peter Terrace. Reprinted by permission of Peter Terrace. English words © 2002 Pearson Education, Inc. 22: "Tie Me Kangaroo Down, Sport" Words and music by Rolf Harris. © 1960, 1961 (Renewed 1988, 1989) Castle Music Pty. Ltd. This arrangement © 2001 Castle Music Pty. Ltd. All Rights for the U.S. and Canada Controlled and Administered by Beechwood Music Corp. All Rights Reserved. International Copyright Secured. Used by Permission. 25: "Pay Me My Money Down" from *Hootenanny Song Book*. Collected and adapted by Lydia Parish. Copyright © 1963 (Renewed) Consolidated Music Publishers. International Copyright Secured. All Rights Reserved. Reprinted by Permission. 26: "We Go Together" from *Grease*. Words and music by Warren Casey and Jim Jacobs. © 1971, 1972 WARREN CASEY and JIM JACOBS. This arrangement © 2001 WARREN CASEY and JIM JACOBS. Copyright Renewed. All Rights Reserved. Used by Permission. 36: "Rock Island Line" New Words and new music arrangement by Huddie Ledbetter. Edited with new additional material by Alan Lomax. TRO–© Copyright 1959 (Renewed) Folkways Music Publishers, Inc., New York, New York. Used by permission. 38: "River" Words and music by Bill Staines. © 1988 Mineral River Music (BMI) Administered by Bug Music. All Rights Reserved. Used by Permission. 41: "Hashewie," (Going Round) from *Roots and Branches*. Courtesy World Music Press. 42: "Riquirrán" Translated by J. Olcutt Sanders. 45: "Eh, Cumpari!"(Hey, Buddy!) by Julius LaRosa and Archie Bleyer. Memory Lane Music Corporation, 1990. Used by permission. 48: "My Home's Across the Blue Ridge Mountains" from *Play It Again Daddy* by Doug Trantham. 50: "The Happy Wanderer" by Friedrich W. Möller and Antonia Ridge, 1954. Sam Fox Publishing Company Inc. Used with permission. 52: "Hey, m'tswala" from *The Melody Book* by Patricia Hackett, © 1991. Reprinted by permission of Prentice-Hall, Inc., Upper Saddle River, NJ. 54: "Osamu kosamu" (Biting Wind) Japanese Folk Song. Translation © 1993 Gloria J. Kiester. Used by permission. 60: "See the Children Playin'" © 2000 Reijiro Music, ASCAP. 62: "Turn the World Around" Words and music by Harry Belafonte and Robert Freedman. Published by Clara Music Publishing Corp. (ASCAP) Administered by Next Decade Entertainment, Inc. All Rights Reserved. Used by Permission. 62: "So Is Life" Words and music by Harry Belafonte and Robert Freedman. Published by Clara Music Publishing Corp. (ASCAP) Administered by Next Decade Entertainment, Inc. All Rights Reserved. Used by Permission. 62: "Do You Know Who I Am?" Words and music by Harry Belafonte and Robert Freedman. Published by Clara Music Publishing Corp. (ASCAP) Administered by Next Decade Entertainment, Inc. All Rights Reserved. Used by Permission. 66: "Ochimbo" English words © 1995 Silver Burdett Ginn. 67: "Straighten Up and Fly Right," Words and music by Nat King Cole and Irving Mills. Copyright 1944 (renewed) by EMI Mills Music, Inc. All Rights Reserved. Reprinted by permission of WARNER BROS. PUBLICATIONS U.S. Inc., Miami, FL 33014 70: "T'hola T'hola" (Softly, Softly) from *African Roots* by Jerry Silverman New York: Chelsea House Publishers. 72: "The Lion Sleeps Tonight", new lyrics and revised music by George David Weiss, Hugo Peretti, and Luigi Creatore. © 1961 Folkways Music Publishers, Inc. © Renewed by George David Weiss, Luigi Creatore, and June Peretti. © Assigned to Abilene Music, Inc. All Rights Reserved. Used by Permission. WARNER BROS. PUBLICATIONS U.S. INC., Miami, FL 33014. 73: "Ala Da'lona" English words © 1995 Silver Burdett Ginn 74: "Cumberland Gap" adapted by Jill Trinka © 1996 Jill Trinka. All rights reserved. Used by permission. 76: "Over the Rainbow" Words by E.Y. Harburg and music by Harold Arlen. 1938 (Renewed © 1966) Metro-Goldwyn-Mayer Inc. 1939 (Renewed © 1967) EMI Feist Catalog Inc. All Rights Reserved. Used by Permission. WARNER BROS. PUBLICATIONS U.S. INC., Miami, FL 33014. 78: "Cantando mentiras" (Singing Tall Tales) from *Cantemos en Espanol* by The Krones. © 1961 Beatrice and Max Krone, Neil A. Kjos Music Co., Publisher. Used by permission of the publisher. English words © 2002 Pearson Education, Inc. 80: "Ode to Joy" (Come and Sing), words by Georgette LeNorth. Used by permission of the author. 87: "At the Hop" Words and music by John Medora, Arthur Singer, and David White. © 1957 Singular Publishing Co. Renewed by Arc Music Corp. and Six Continents. All Rights Reserved. Used by Permission. 90: "Santa Clara" English words © 1998 Silver Burdett Ginn. 92: "Doraji"(Bluebells) English words © 1995 Silver Burdett Ginn. 93: "La Tarara" English words © 2002 Pearson Education, Inc. 94: "Old House, Tear It Down!" African American Folk Song Collected by John Work. 96: "Kookaburra" Words and music by Marion Sinclair. 96: "Missy-La, Massa-La" from *Brown Girl in the Ring* by Alan Lomax. Copyright © 1997 by Alan Lomax. Reprinted by permission of Pantheon Books, a division of Random House, Inc. 98: "The Computer," Words by Fitzhugh Dodson. Music © 2002 Pearson Education, Inc. 100: "Do Wah Diddy Diddy" by Jeff Barry and Ellie Greenwich, © 1963, 1964 (Copyrights Renewed) Trio Music Co. Inc. and Universal-Songs of Polygram International, Inc. This arrangement © 2001 Trio Music Co. Inc. and Universal-Songs of Polygram International, Inc. All Rights Reserved. Used by permission. WARNER BROS. PUBLICATIONS U. S. INC., Miami, FL 33014, and Hal Leonard Corporation. 101: "I Believe I Can Fly". Words and music by R. Kelly. Copyright © 1996 by Zomba Songs Inc. and R. Kelly Publishing, Inc. (adm. by Zomba Songs, Inc.). All Rights Reserved. Reprinted by permission of WARNER BROS. PUBLICATIONS U.S. Inc., Miami, FL 33014. 106: "Freedom" from *Shenandoah*. Words by Peter Udell, music by Gary Geld. © 1974, 1975 Gary Geld and Peter Udell. This arrangement © 2001 Gary Geld and Peter Udell. All rights controlled by Edwin H. Morris & Company, A Division of MPL Communications, Inc. All rights Reserved. Used by Permission. 108: "El rancho grande" (The Big Ranch) Silvano Ramos © 1927 Edward B. Marks Music Company. Copyright renewed. Used by permission. All rights reserved. English words © 2002 Pearson Education, Inc. 112: "Minka" English words © 1971 Silver Burdett. 114: "Tancovacka" (Dancing) Czech words © 2002 Pearson Education, Inc. 116: "Los niños en España cantan" (In Spain the Children Sing) Folk song from Mexico, English words by S.T. 116: "Let Music Surround You" by Fran Smartt Addicott, 1986. Used by permission. 119: "Theme from NEW YORK, NEW YORK" by John Kander and Fred Ebo. © 1977 United Artists Corporation. All Rights Controlled by EMI Unart Catalog Inc. All Rights Reserved. Used by Permission. WARNER BROS. PUBLICATIONS U.S. INC., Miami, FL 33014. 124: "Blow, Ye Winds", from *Songs of American Sailormen* by Joanne C. Colcord. Copyright 1938 by W.W. Norton & Co. Inc. Used by permission of W.W. Norton & Co, Inc. 130: "Follow the Drinkin' Gourd" © 1995 Silver Burdett Ginn 132: "Cielito lindo" English words © 1995 Silver Burdett Ginn. 135: "Route 66" Words and music by Bobby Troup. Copyright © 1946, Renewed © 1973, Assigned 1974 to Londontown Music. This arrangement copyright © 2001 Londontown Music. All Rights outside the U.S.A. controlled by E.H. Morris & Company. International Copyright Secured. All Rights Reserved. Used by Permission. 139: "California, Here I Come" Words and music by Al Jolson, B. G. Desylva, and Joseph Meyer. © 1924 (Renewed) Warner Bros. Inc. Rights for Extended Renewal Term in U. S. controlled by Warner Bros. Inc., Stephen Ballentine Music and Meyer-JoRo Music. All Rights Reserved. Used by Permission. WARNER BROS. PUBLICATIONS U.S. INC., Miami, FL 33014. 140: "Pastures of Plenty" Words and music by Woody Guthrie. TRO–© Copyright 1960 (Renewed) 1963 (Renewed) Ludlow Music, Inc., New York, New York. Used by permission. 142: "Ai Dunaii Moy," (Ah, My Belov'd Dunaii) folk song from Russia, English version Charles Haywood. 144: "Tina singu" Transcribed from the singing of Kathleen Hill from *Chansons de Notre Chalet*. Copyright © 1957 Cooperative Recreation Service, Inc. 146: "La raspa" English words © 1995 Silver Burdett Ginn. 149: "Shri Ram, jai Ram" © 1958, C.R.S. Transferred to World Around Songs 1976, 20 Colberts Crk. Burnsville, NC 28714. Used with permission. 152: "Xiao" (Bamboo Flute) © 1995 Silver Burdett Ginn. 154: "Wings of a Dove" © Berandol Music Publishers. Reprinted by permission. 156: "Love Can Build a Bridge" Words and music by Paul Overstreet, Naomi Judd, and John Jarvis. Copyright © 1990 Scarlet Moon Music, Inc. (administered by Copyright Management

(Continued on page 254)

Contents

Accompaniments 4
Song Index 255

To the Teacher

Keyboard accompaniments are provided for those songs for which the keyboard is an appropriate instrument or a reasonable substitute for authentic instruments.

The triangle-shaped boxes within an accompaniment designate the beginnings of lines of music on the student page. Harmonies in an accompaniment may differ from those on the recording and from the chord symbols in the student text.

Student Page 2

Turn the Beat Around

Words and Music by Peter Jackson Jr., and Gerald Jackson
Arranged by Buddy Skipper

Student Page 6

Put a Little Love in Your Heart

*Words and Music by Jimmy Holiday,
Randy Myers, and Jackie De Shannon
Arranged by Buddy Skipper*

10

Soldier, Soldier

Haul Away, Joe

Sea shantey from England
Arranged by Buddy Skipper

2. Oh, once I was in Ireland diggin' turf and 'taties, . . .
   But now I'm on a lime-juice ship hauling on the braces, . . .

3. King Louie was the King of France before the revolution, . . .
   King Louie got his head cut off which spoiled his constitution, . . .

6
Melody
si - rov - nig, nakh - shoun ga - ka - vik.
Pret - ty par - tridge, love - ly bird, greet - ing you and me.

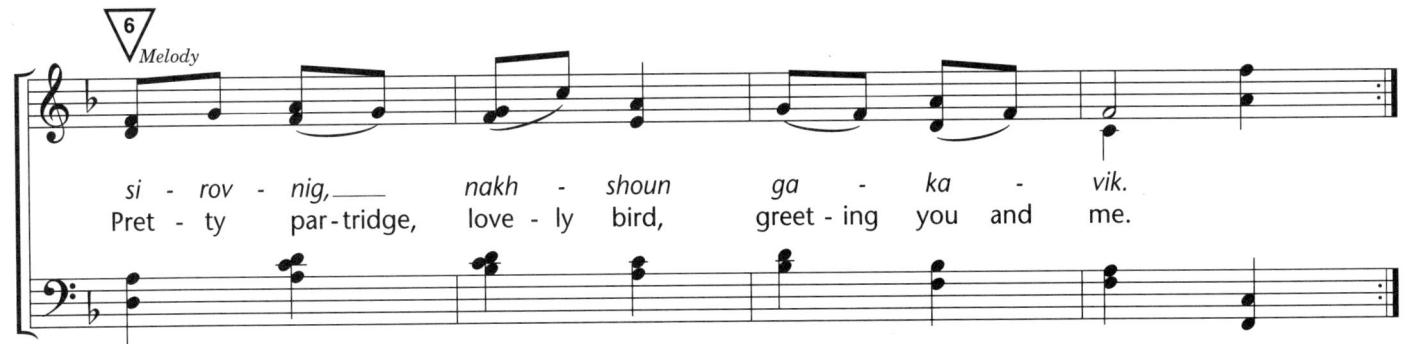

Student Page 23

Tsuki (The Moon)

English Words by Kazuo Akiyama

School Song from Japan
Arranged by Carol Jay

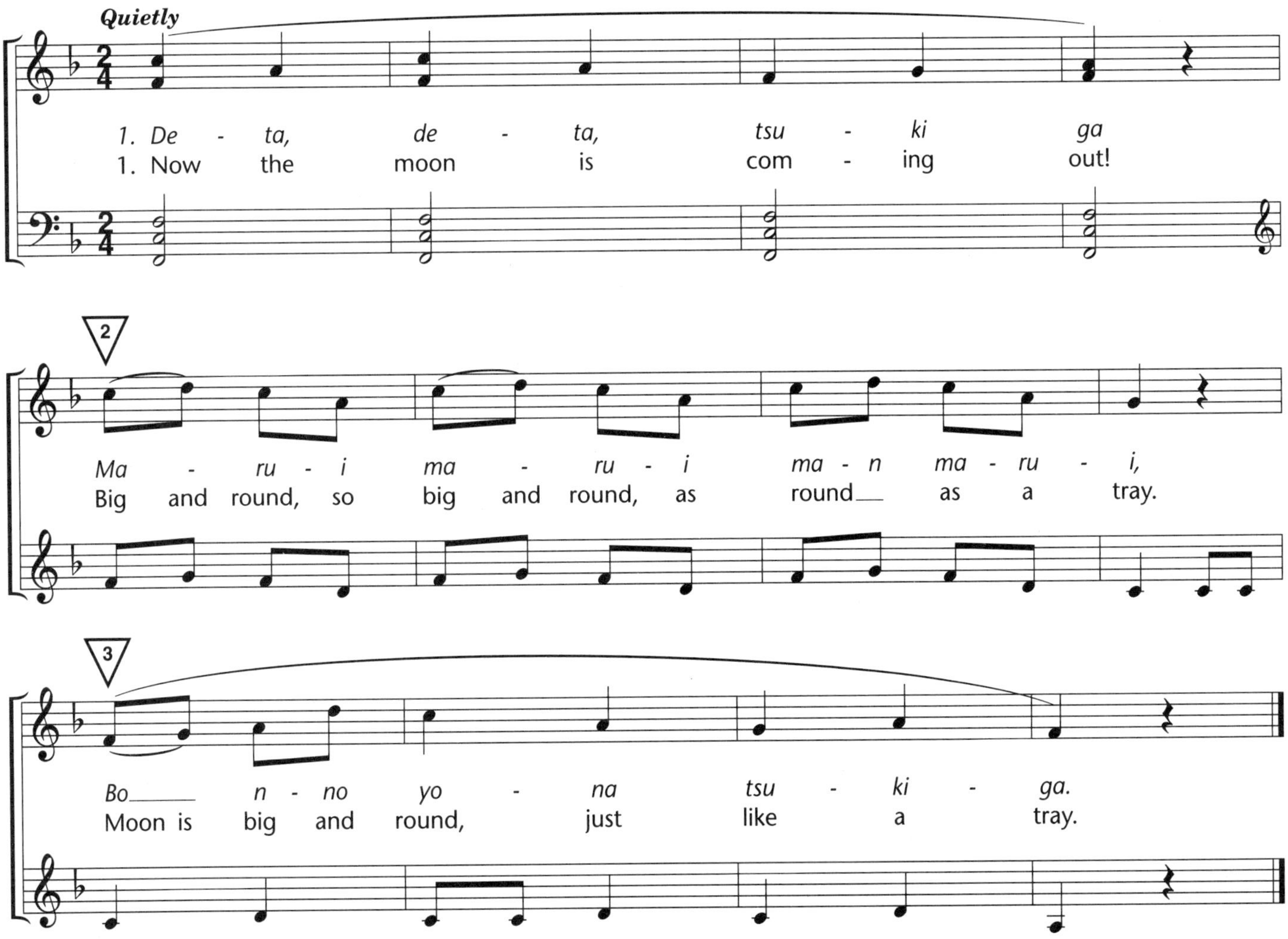
Quietly
1. De - ta, de - ta, tsu - ki ga
1. Now the moon is com - ing out!
2
Ma - ru - i ma - ru - i ma - n ma - ru - i,
Big and round, so big and round, as round as a tray.
3
Bo n - no yo - na tsu - ki - ga.
Moon is big and round, just like a tray.

2. *Kaku reta kumoni,*
Kuroi, kuroi makuroi,
Sumino yona kumoni.

2. Now the moon is hiding,
Gone away, O gone away, O gone away so far.
Up behind the clouds as black as tar.

Limbo Like Me

"Limbo Like Me" New words and new music adapted by Massie Patterson and Sammy Heyward. (Based on a traditional song) TRO-© 1963 (Renewed) Ludlow Music, Inc., New York, NY. Used by permission.

Gonna Ride Up in the Chariot

African American Spiritual
Arranged by W. R. Colbrook

2. Gonna meet my brother there, yes, Soon-a in the mornin',
   Meet my brother there, yes, Soon-a in the mornin',
   Meet my brother there, yes, Soon-a in the mornin',
   And I hope I'll join the band. *Refrain*

3. Gonna chatter with the angels, Soon-a in the mornin',
   Chatter with the angels, Soon-a in the mornin',
   Chatter with the angels, Soon-a in the mornin',
   And I hope I'll join the band. *Refrain*

Waitin' for the Light to Shine from BIG RIVER

Words and Music by Roger Miller
Arranged by John Girt

Tie Me Kangaroo Down, Sport

3. Take me koala back, Jack.
   Take me koala back.
   He lives somewhere on the track, Mac.
   So take me koala back.
   All together now! *Refrain*

4. Mind me platypus duck, Bill.
   Mind me platypus duck.
   Don't let him go running amok, Bill.
   So mind me platypus duck.
   All together now! *Refrain*

5. Play your didgeridoo, Blue.
   Play your didgeridoo.
   Keep playing 'til I shoot thro', Blue.
   Play your didgeridoo.
   All together now! *Refrain*

6. Tan me hide when I'm dead, Fred.
   Tan me hide when I'm dead.
   So we tanned his hide when he died, Clyde.
   And that's it hanging on the shed.
   All together now! *Refrain*

I'm Gonna Sing

African American Spiritual
Arranged by Carmino Ravosa

2. I'm gonna shout when the spirit says "Shout," *(3 times)*
   And obey the spirit of the Lord.

3. I'm gonna pray when the spirit says "Pray," *(3 times)*
   And obey the spirit of the Lord.

4. I'm gonna sing when the spirit says "Sing," *(3 times)*
   And obey the spirit of the Lord.

Pay Me My Money Down

Work Song from the Georgia Sea Islands
Collected and Adapted by Lydia A. Parrish
Arranged by Francis Girard

3. Well, I wish I was Mr. Steven's son,
   "Pay me my money down,"
   Sit on the bank and watch the work done,
   "Pay me my money down."   *Refrain*

Student Page 42

We Go Together

Lyrics and Music by Warren Casey and Jim Jacobs
Arranged by Buddy Skipper

Copyright © 1971, 1972, 1985 WARREN CASEY and JIM JACOBS. All Rights Throughout the World Controlled by EDWIN H. MORRIS & COMPANY, A Division of MPL Communications, Inc., International Copyright Secured. All Rights Reserved.

Oh, Danny Boy

Words by Thomas Moore

Folk Song from Ireland
Arranged by Buddy Skipper

Sadly

1. Oh, Danny Boy, the pipes, the pipes are calling, From glen to glen, and down the mountainside; The summer's gone, and all the roses falling, 'Tis you, 'tis you must go, and I must bide. But come ye back when summer's in the meadow, Or when the valley's hushed and white with

2. But when you come and all the flow'rs are dying, If I am dead, as dead I well may be; You'll come and find the place where I am lying, And kneel and say an Ave there for me. And I shall hear, tho' soft you tread above me, And all my grave will warmer, sweeter

Somebody's Knockin' at Your Door

African American Spiritual
Arranged by Elsie Plant

Student Page 51

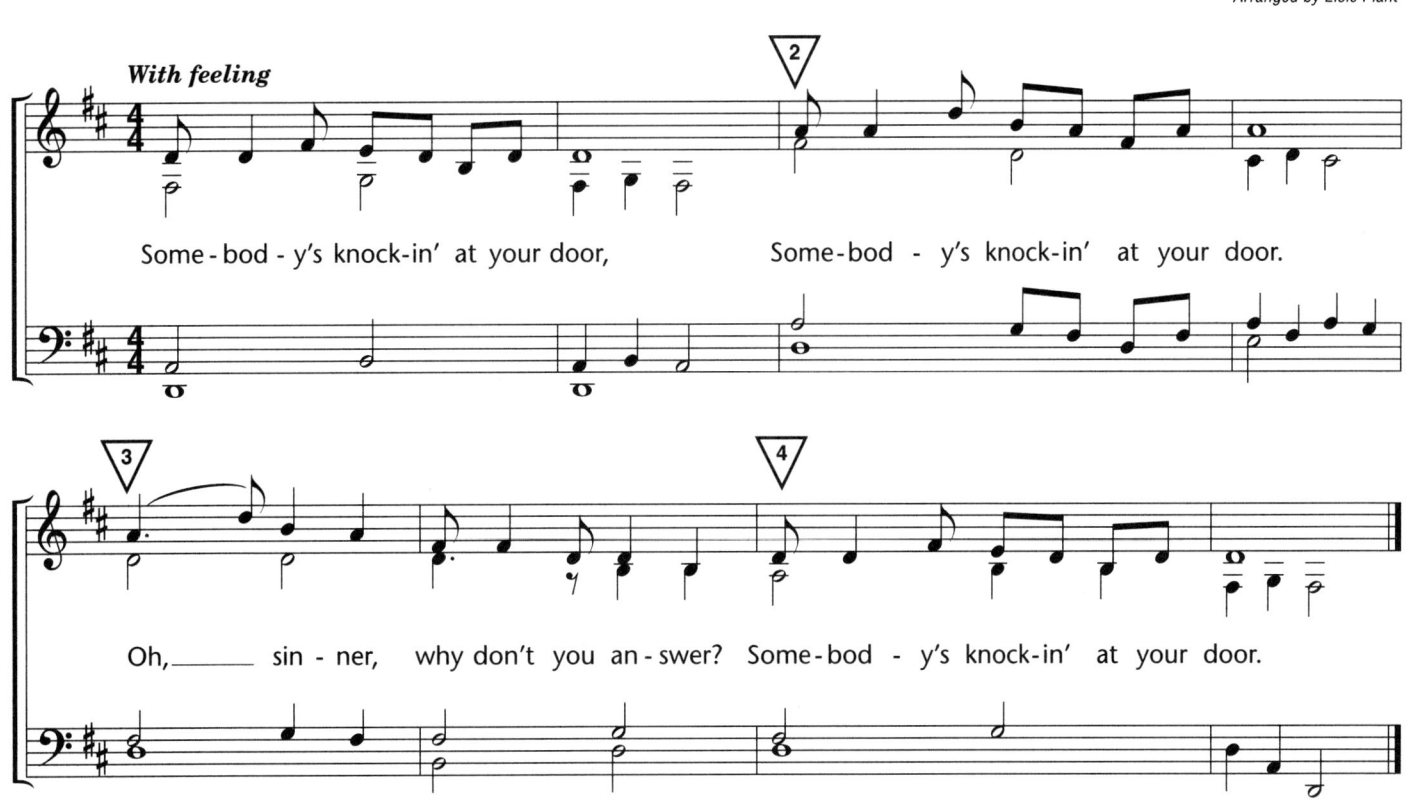

Student Page 52

Rock Island Line

Edited with New Additional Material by Alan Lomax

Railroad Song
New Words and Arrangement by Huddie Ledbetter
Arranged by Bill Wallace

"Rock Island Line" New words and new music arrangement by Huddie Ledbetter. Edited with new additional material by Alan Lomax. TRO - © Copyright 1959 (Renewed) Folkways Music Publishers, Inc., New York, New York. Used by permission.

Riquirrán

Sourwood Mountain

Folk Song from the Appalachian Mountains
Arranged by Anita P. Davis

2. My true love's
    a blue-eyed daisy, Hey, . . .
   If I don't get her
    I'll go crazy, Hey, . . .
   Big dogs bark
    and little ones bite you, Hey, . . .
   Big girls court
    and little ones slight you, Hey, . . .

3. My true love
    lives by the river, Hey, . . .
   A few more jumps
    and I'll be with her, Hey, . . .
   My true love
    lives up in the hollow, Hey, . . .
   She won't come
    and I won't follow, Hey, . . .

Eh, cumpari! (Hey, Buddy!)

Words and Music by Julius La Rosa and Archie Bleyer
Arranged by Buddy Skipper

4. . . . 'U viulinu? . . .
5. . . . A la trumbetta? . . .
6. . . . A la trombona? . . .

4. . . . the violin? . . .
5. . . . the brassy trumpet? . . .
6. . . . the slide trombone?

Student Page 82

My Home's Across the Blue Ridge Mountains

Collected by Louis Land Bascom

Folk Song from the Southern United States
Arranged by Carol Jay

Student Page 74

Canoe Song

Words and Music by Margaret E. McGhee
Arranged by Rene LeClair

Brightly

1. My pad - dle's keen and bright, Flash - ing with sil - ver,
2. Dip, dip and swing her back, Flash - ing with sil - ver,

Fol - low the wild goose flight, Dip, dip and swing.
Fol - low the wild goose track, Dip, dip and swing.

Student Page 77

Hey, m'tswala

Folk Song from Africa
Arranged by Christopher Hatcher

Steadily

Hey, m'tswa - la, ne - ye ti - pa sa - me tswa - la.

Paw-Paw Patch

Play-Party Song from the United States
Arranged by Cameron McGraw

Ōsamu kosamu (Biting Wind)

English Words by Gloria J. Kiester

Folk Song from Japan
Arranged by John Detroy

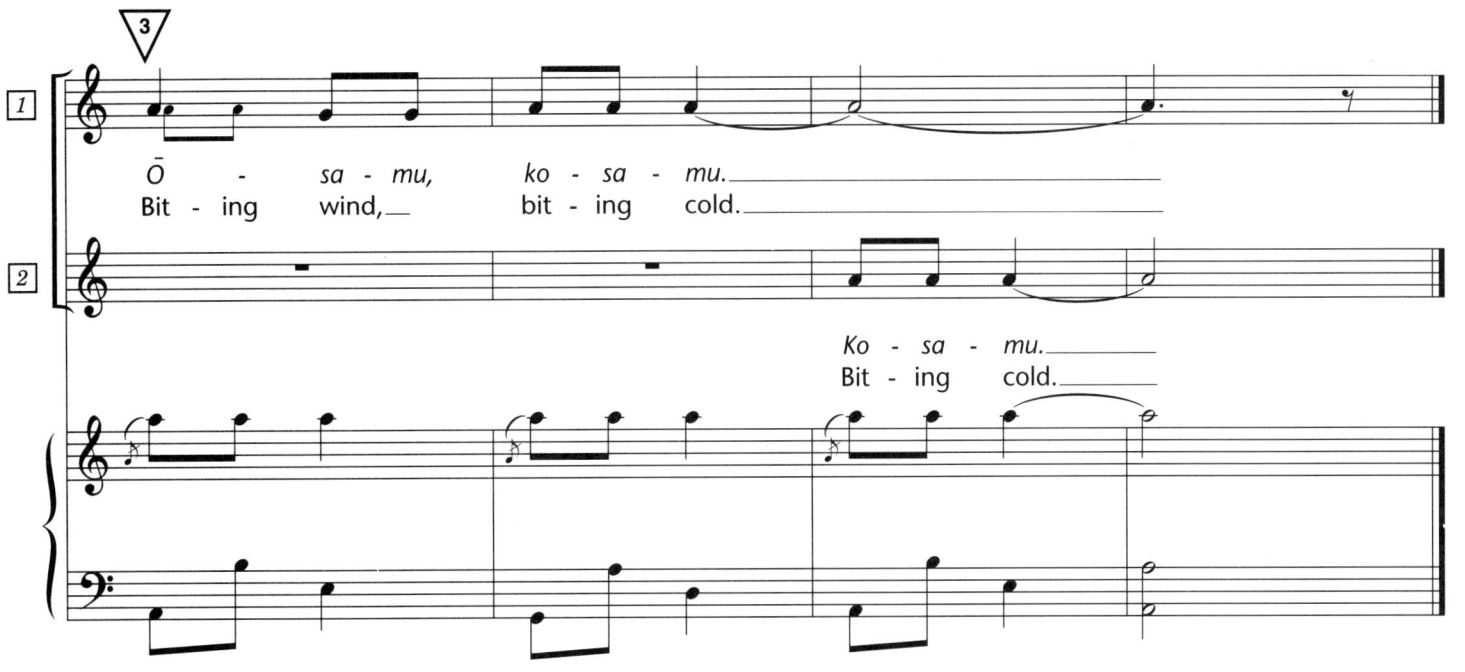

Rise and Shine

Folk Song from the United States
Arranged by Marilyn J. Patterson

First time: G
Second time: B

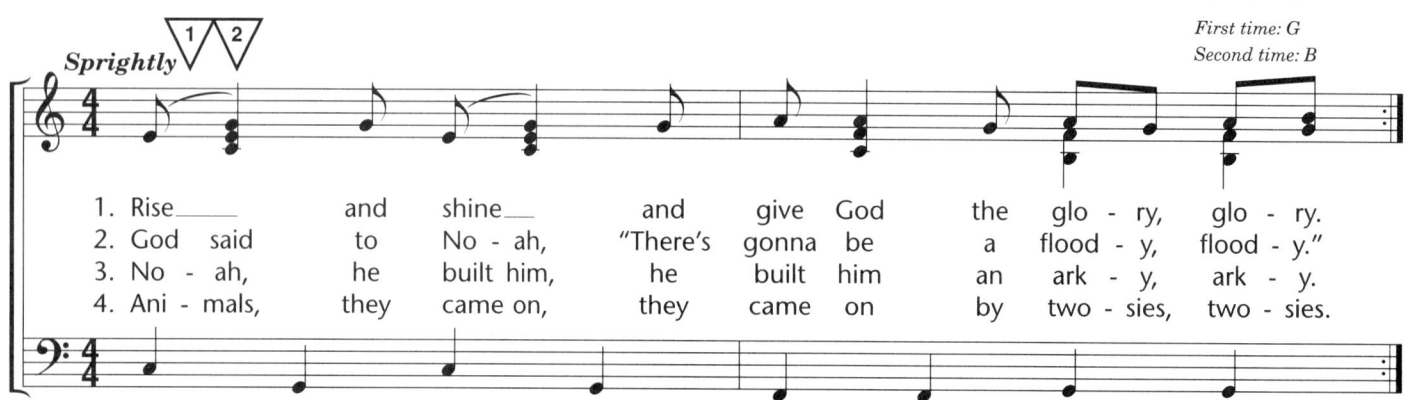
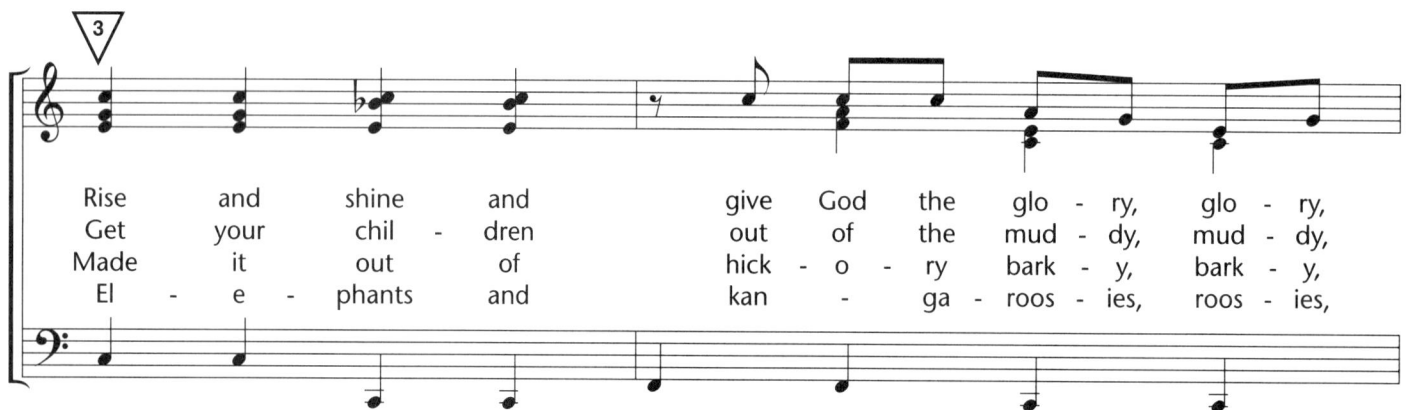

5. Rained and rained
   for forty daysies, daysies.
   Rained and rained
   for forty daysies, daysies.
   Nearly drove those animals crazy, crazy,...

6. Noah, he sent out,
   he sent out a dovey, dovey.
   Noah, he sent out,
   he sent out a dovey, dovey.
   Sent him to the heavens abovey, bovey,...

7. Sun came out
   and dried off the landy, landy.
   Sun came out
   and dried off the landy, landy.
   Ev'rything was fine and dandy, dandy,...

8. This is the end,
   the end of my story, story.
   This is the end,
   the end of my story, story.
   Ev'rything is hunky-dory, dory,...

Weevily Wheat

Son macaron

Traditional
Arranged by Marilyn J. Patterson

4. Water make the river,
river wash the mountain,
Fire make the sunlight,
turn the world around.

5. Heart is of the river
body is the mountain,
Spirit is the sunlight,
turn the world around.

6. We are of the spirit,
truly can the spirit,
Only can the spirit,
turn the world around.

Student Page 114

Over My Head

African American Spiritual
Arranged by Rosemary Jacques

Ochimbo

English Words by Margaret Marks

Folk Song from Kenya
As Sung by Ruth Nthreketha
Arranged by Mark A. Miller

Straighten Up and Fly Right

Words and Music by Nat King Cole and Irving Mills
Arranged by John Girt

Student Page 124

T'hola, t'hola (Softly, Softly)

Folk Song from Africa
Arranged by Christopher Hatcher

Student Page 127

The Lion Sleeps Tonight (Wimoweh)(Mbube)

Words and Revised Music by George David Weiss, Hugo Peretti, and Luigi Creatore
Arranged by John Girt

Student Page 132

Ala Da´lona

English Words by Alice Firgau

Folk Song from Arabia
Arranged by Alice Firgau

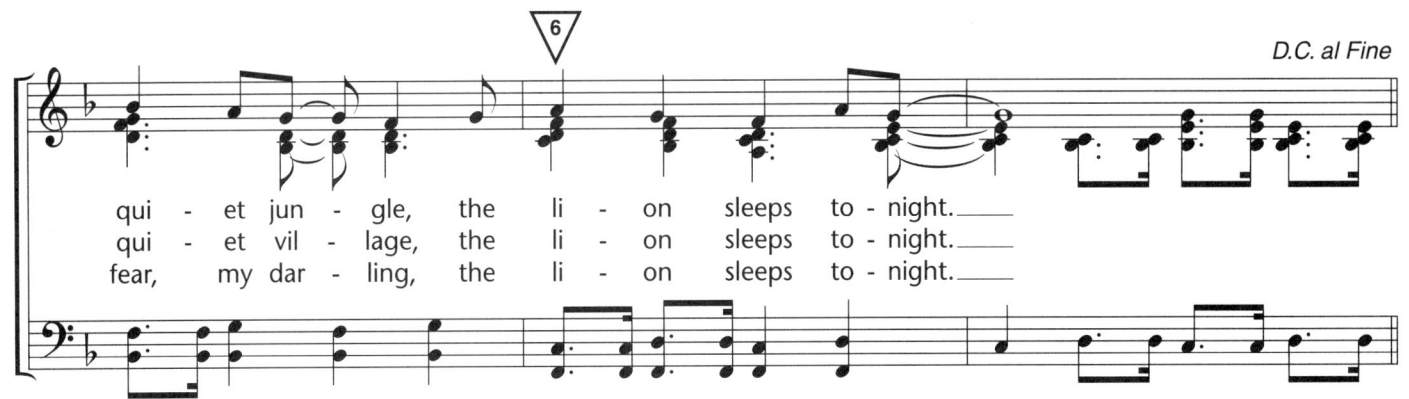

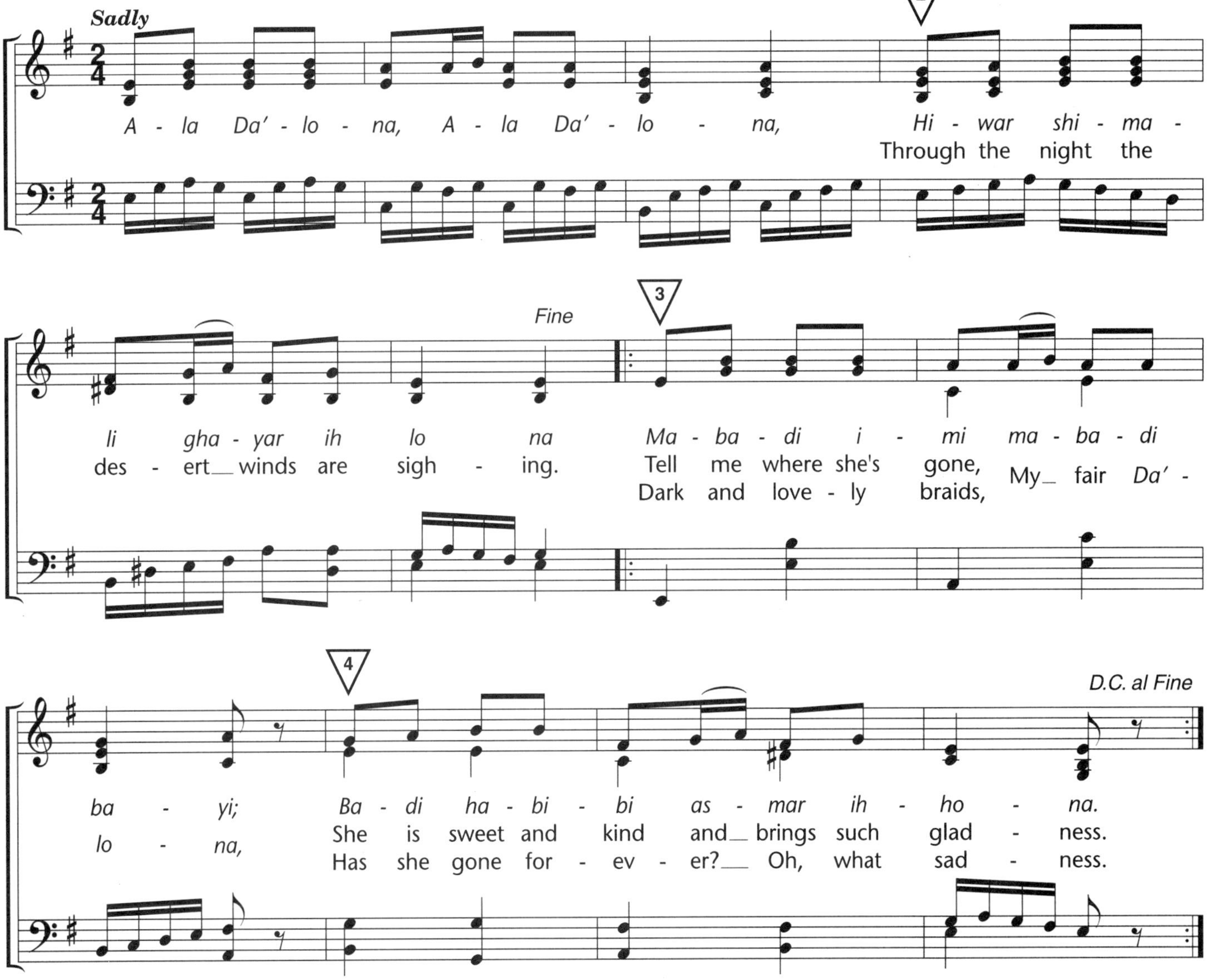

Cumberland Gap

Play-Party Song from Kentucky
Arranged by Martha Hilley

2. Cumberland Gap is a mighty fine place, . . . *(3 times)*
   Three kinds of water to wash your face. *Refrain*

3. Cumberland Gap with its cliffs and rocks, . . . *(3 times)*
   Home of the panther, bear, and fox. *Refrain*

4. Me and my wife and my wife's grandpap, . . . *(3 times)*
   We raise Cain at Cumberland Gap. *Refrain*

Canción de cuna (Cradle Song)

Folk Song from Latin America
Arranged by Mark A. Miller

75

Cantando mentiras (Singing Tall Tales)

English Words by Alice Firgau

Folk Song from Latin America
Arranged by Alice Firgau

Chairs to Mend

Street Call From England
Arranged by John Courant

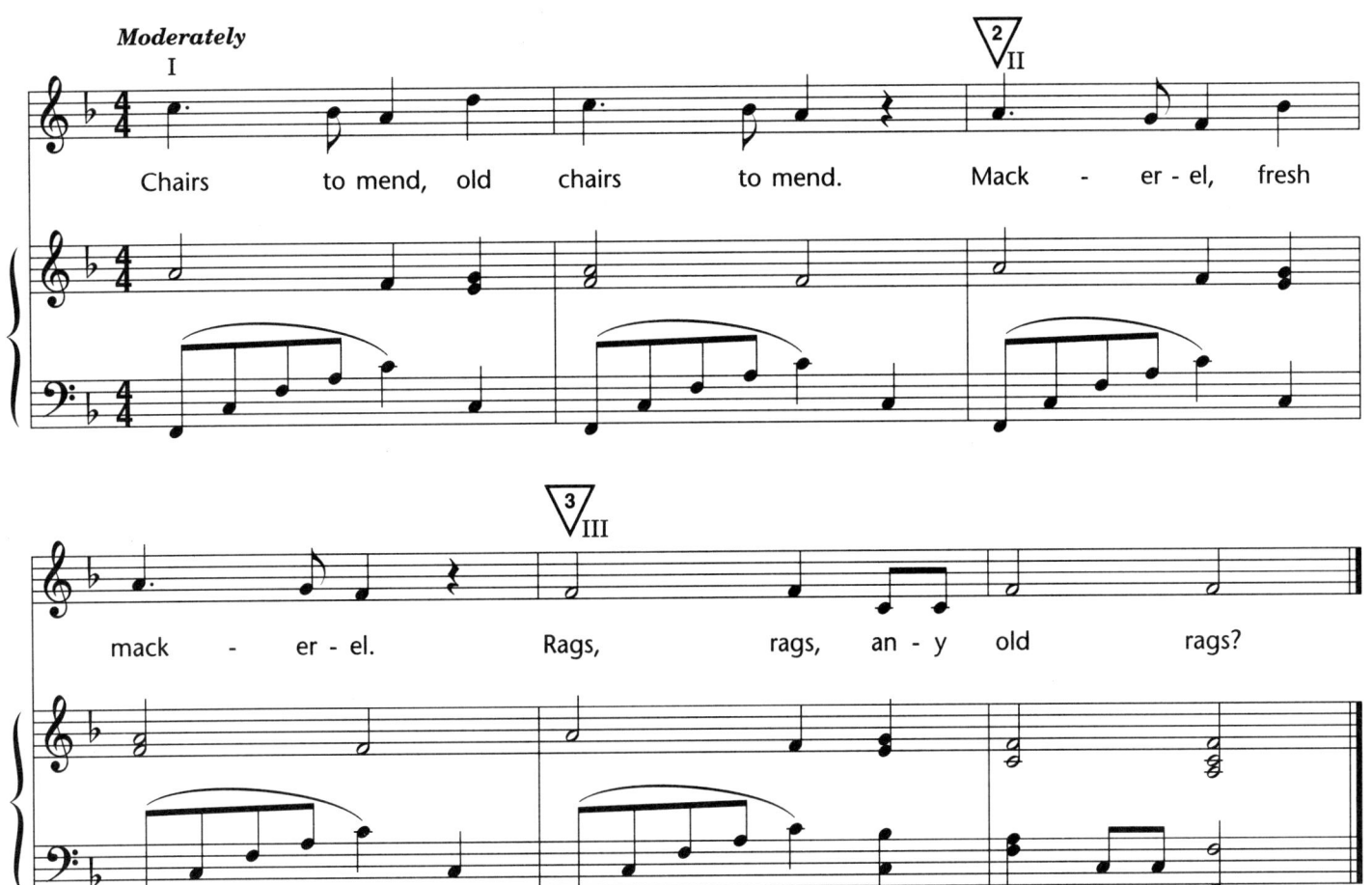

Ode to Joy

Words by Friedrich Schiller
English Words by Georgette LeNorth

Music by Ludwig van Beethoven
Arranged by Alan Seale and Don Kalbach

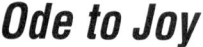

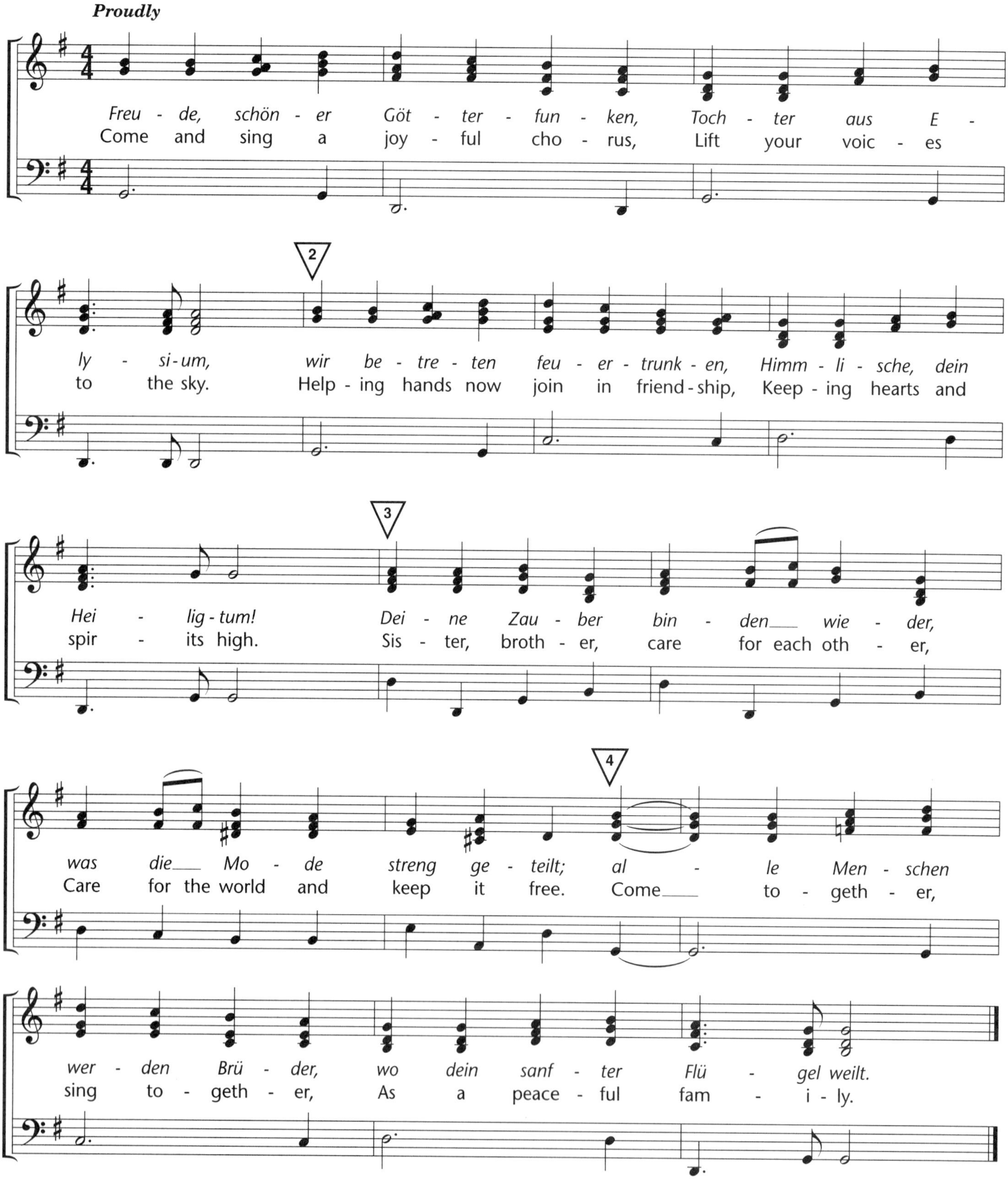

Amazing Grace

Words by John Newton

Early American Melody
Arranged by Frank Fox

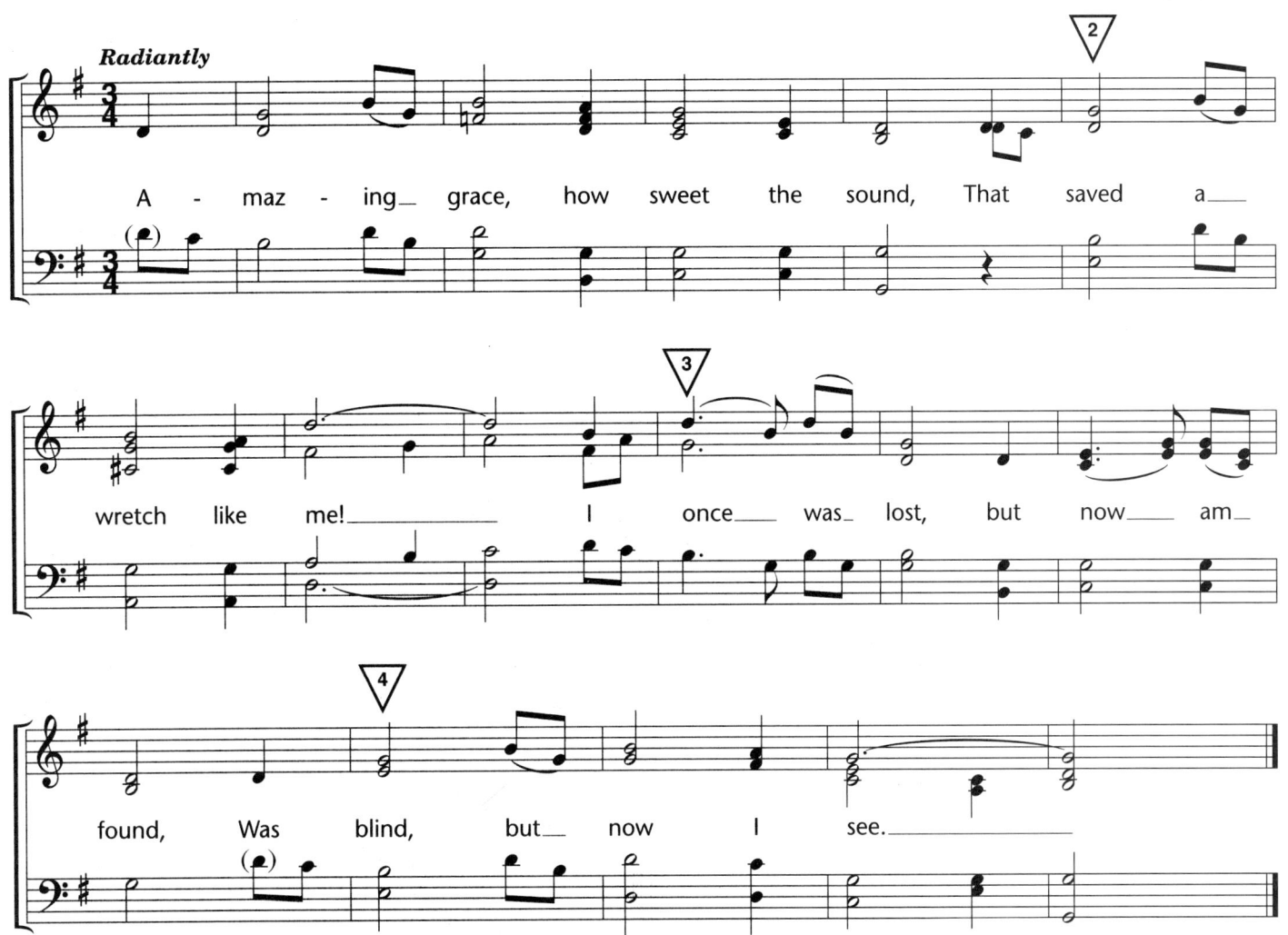

2. 'Twas grace that taught my heart to fear,
And grace my fears relieved;
How precious did that grace appear
The hour I first believed!

3. Through many dangers, toils, and snares,
I have already come;
'Tis grace has brought me safe thus far,
And grace will lead me home.

At the Hop

Words and Music by A. Singer, J. Medora, and D. White
Arranged by Buddy Skipper

Doraji (Bluebells)

English Words by Patricia Shehan Campbell

Folk Song from Korea
Arranged by Bruce Simpson

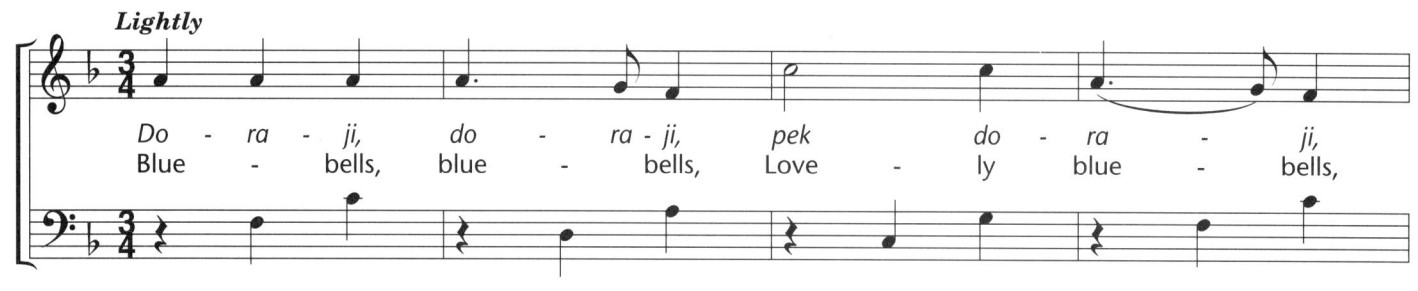

Do - ra - ji, do - ra - ji, pek do - ra - ji,
Blue - bells, blue - bells, Love - ly blue - bells,

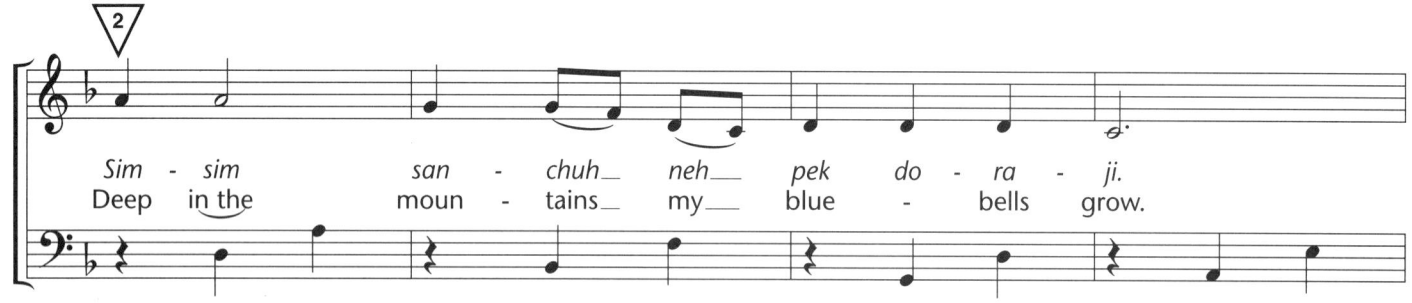

Sim - sim san - chuh neh pek do - ra - ji.
Deep in the moun - tains my blue - bells grow.

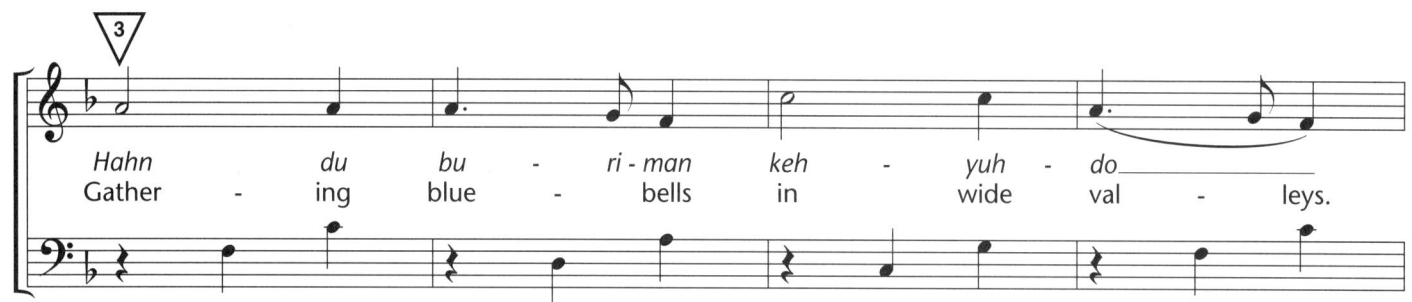

Hahn du bu - ri - man keh - yuh - do
Gather - ing blue - bells in wide val - leys.

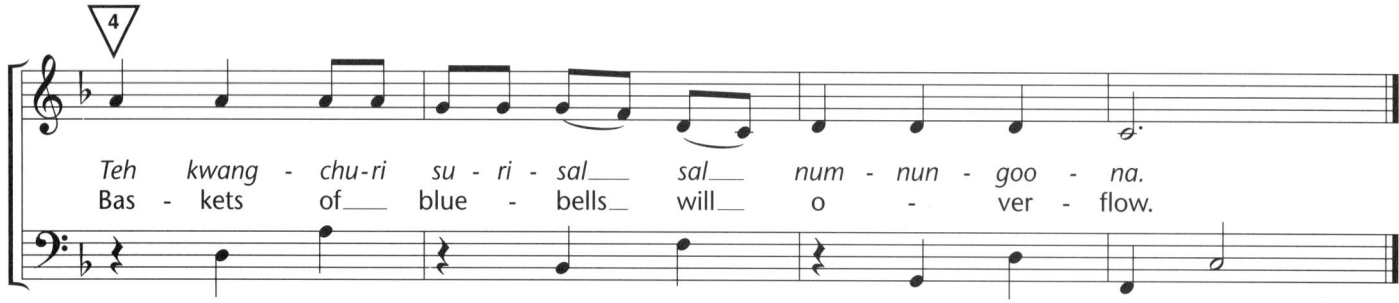

Teh kwang - chu - ri su - ri - sal sal num - nun - goo - na.
Bas - kets of blue - bells will o - ver - flow.

La Tarara

English Words by Alice D. Firgau

Folk Song from Spain
Arranged by Joyce Kalbach

Student Page 174

Old House, Tear It Down!

Collected by John Work

African American Work Song
Arranged by John Girt

All Night, All Day

African American Spiritual
Arranged by James Rooker

Student Page 182

Kookaburra

Words and Music by Marion Sinclair
Arranged by William and Patrick Medley

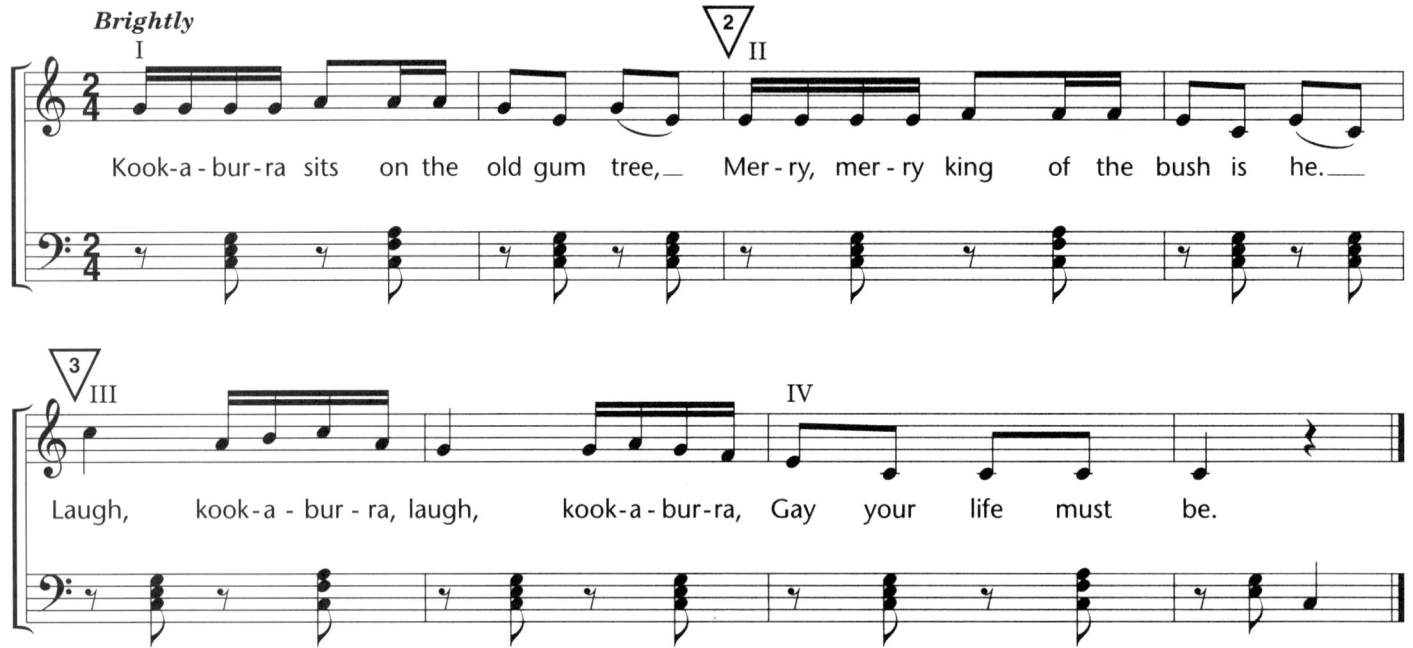

Student Page 184

Missy-La, Massa-La

Game Song from the Caribbean
Arranged by Joyce Kalbach

Student Page 192

Ah, Poor Bird

Traditional Round from England
Arranged by Audrey Schultz

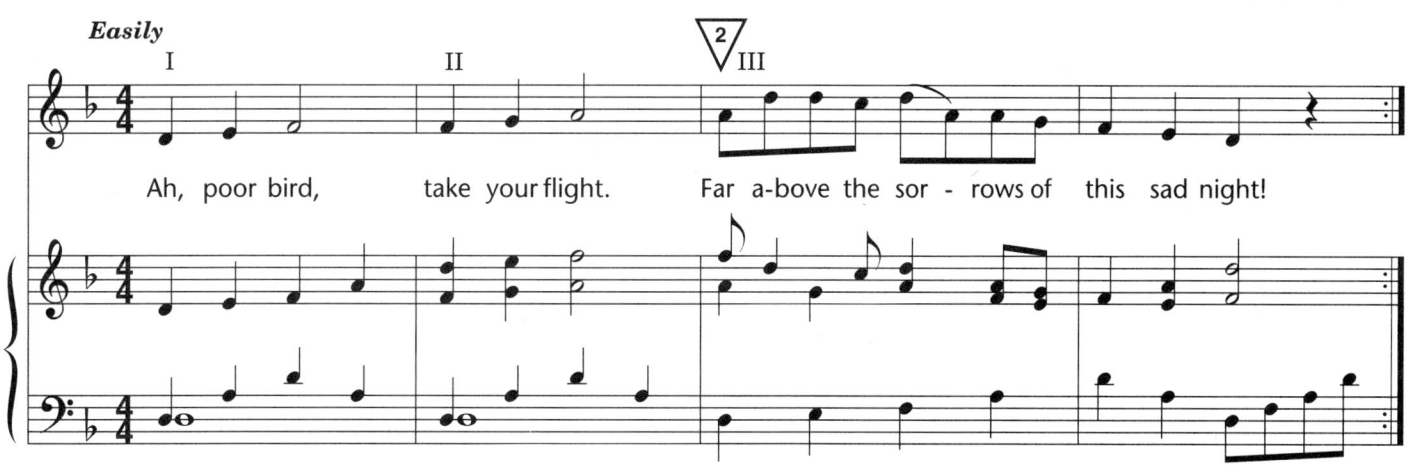

Student Page 193

Liebe ist ein Ring (Love Is Like a Ring)

Traditional Round from Germany
Arranged by Lisa Reed

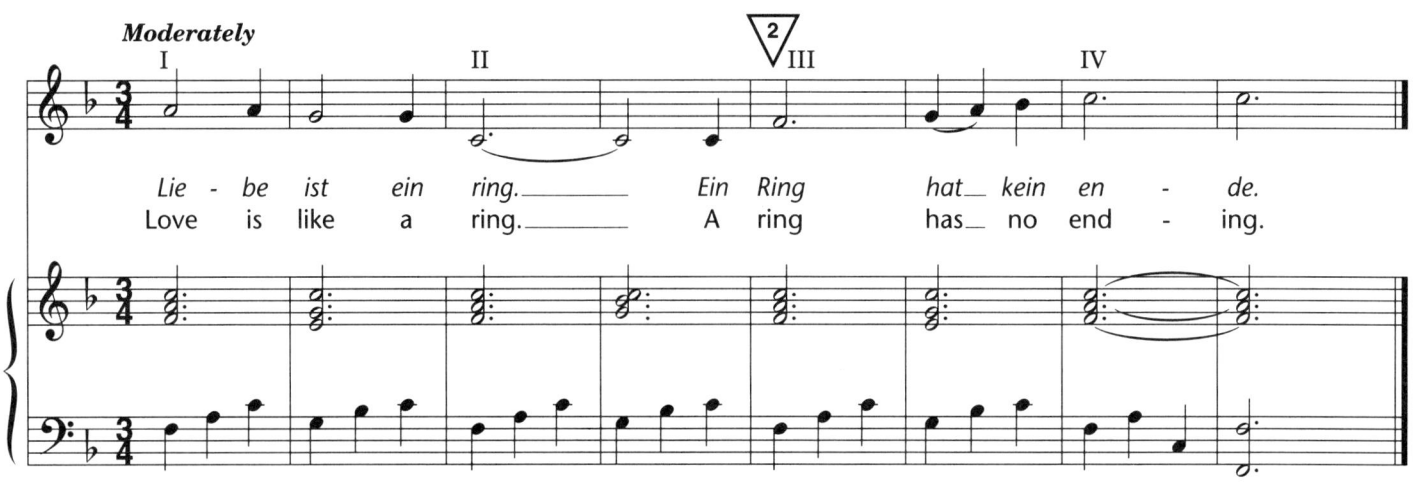

Student Page 195

The Computer

Words by Fitzhugh Dodson

Music by Mary Shamrock
Arranged by Joyce Kalbach

Frog Music

Folk Song from Canada
Arranged by Rosemary Jacques

Student Page 196

Do Wah Diddy Diddy (excerpt)

Words and Music by Jeff Barry and Ellie Greenwich
Arranged by Phil Perkins

I Believe I Can Fly

Words and Music by R. Kelly
Arranged by Buddy Skipper

103

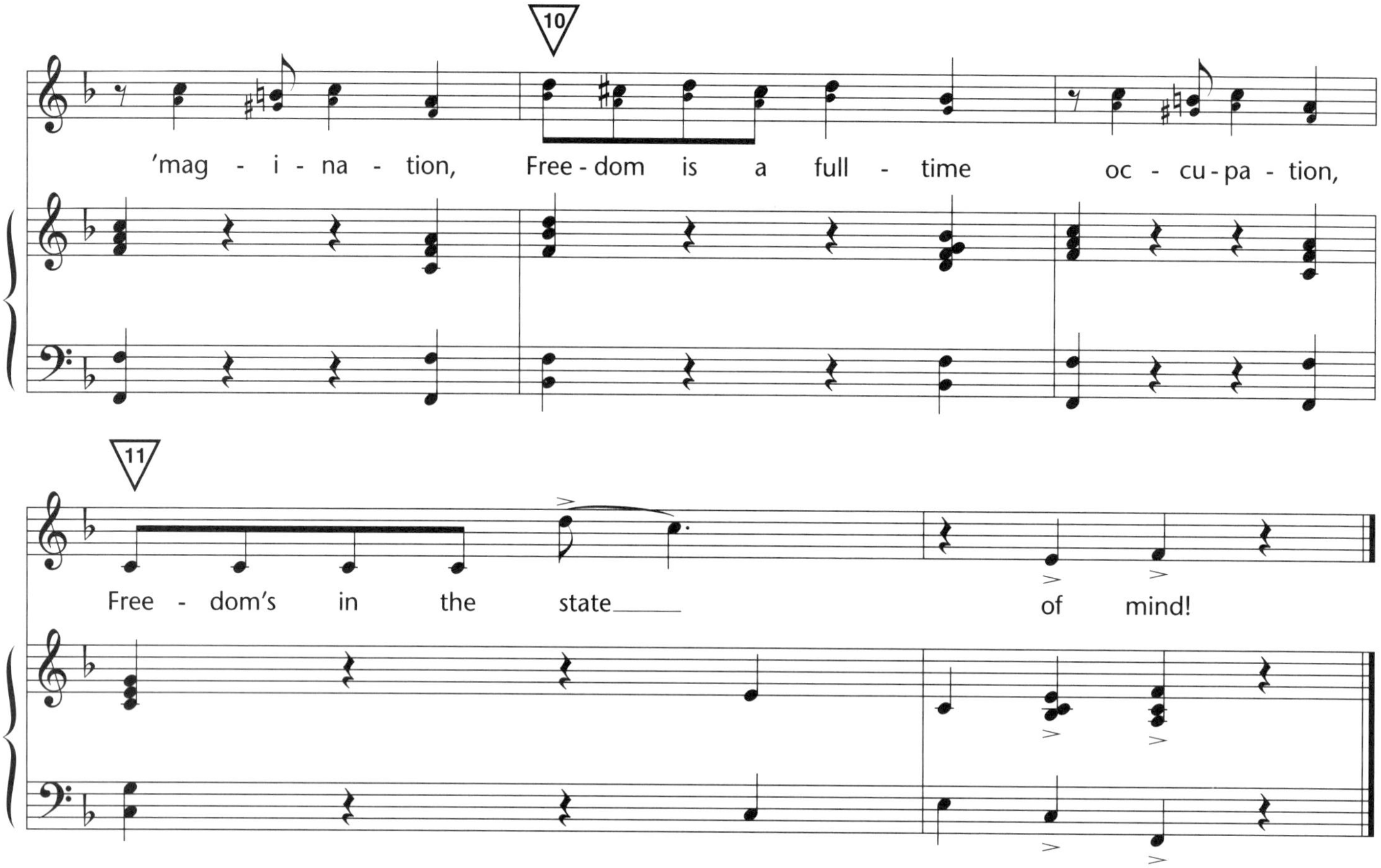

Student Page 211

El rancho grande (The Big Ranch)

English Words by Alice D. Firgau

Music by Silvano R. Ramos
Arranged by William Simon

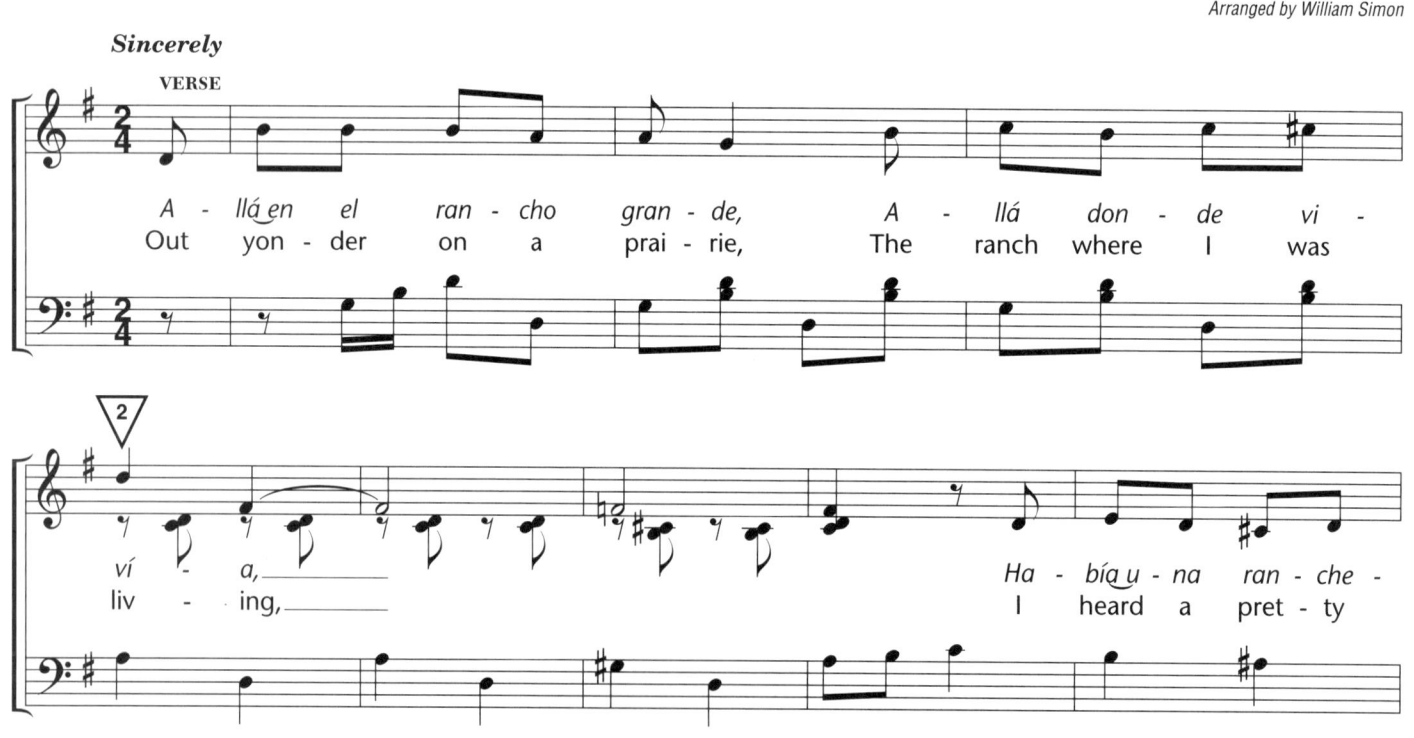

Oh, How Lovely Is the Evening

Traditional German Melody
Arranged by Bruce Simpson

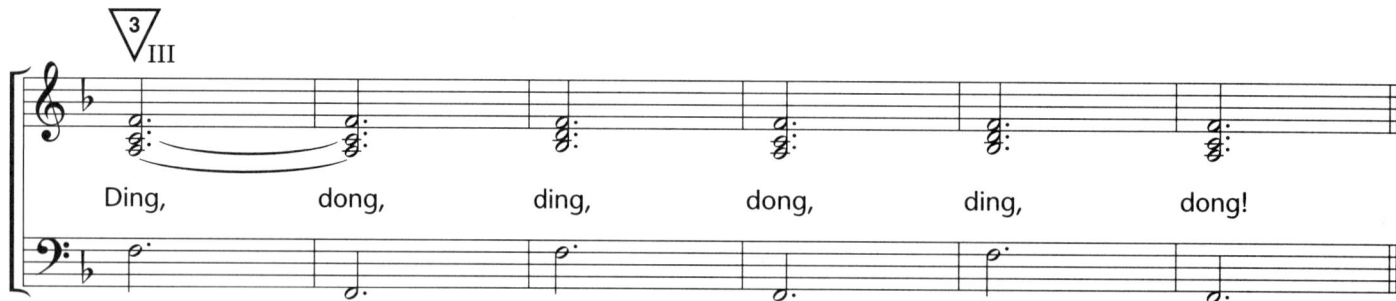

Dry Bones Come Skipping

Traditional Song from the United States
Arranged by John Girt

Minka

English Words by Margaret Marks

Folk Song from Ukraine
Arranged by Paul Beck

Steadily

1. Said the Cos-sack to the maid-en, "Love, my heart is heav-y lad-en.
2. Off the Cos-sack went to bat-tle, All a-lone poor Mink-a sat E-

Du-ty calls, so I'm a-fraid, En-chant-ress, we must part.
lev-en years, and she grew fat, Al-though her heart was true.

I be-seech you, fair-est Mink-a, Wait for me, I hate to think An-
When at last her Cos-sack lov-er Came back home and looked her o-ver,

oth-er man might come and tink-er With your faith-ful heart!"
He be-gan to court an-oth-er. Broke her heart in two!

Thula, thula, ngoana (Sleep, Sleep, Baby)

Folk Song from the Lesotho Region of South Africa
Arranged by Christopher Hatcher

Student Page 230

Frog Round

Traditional Song from the United States
Arranged by Christopher Hatcher

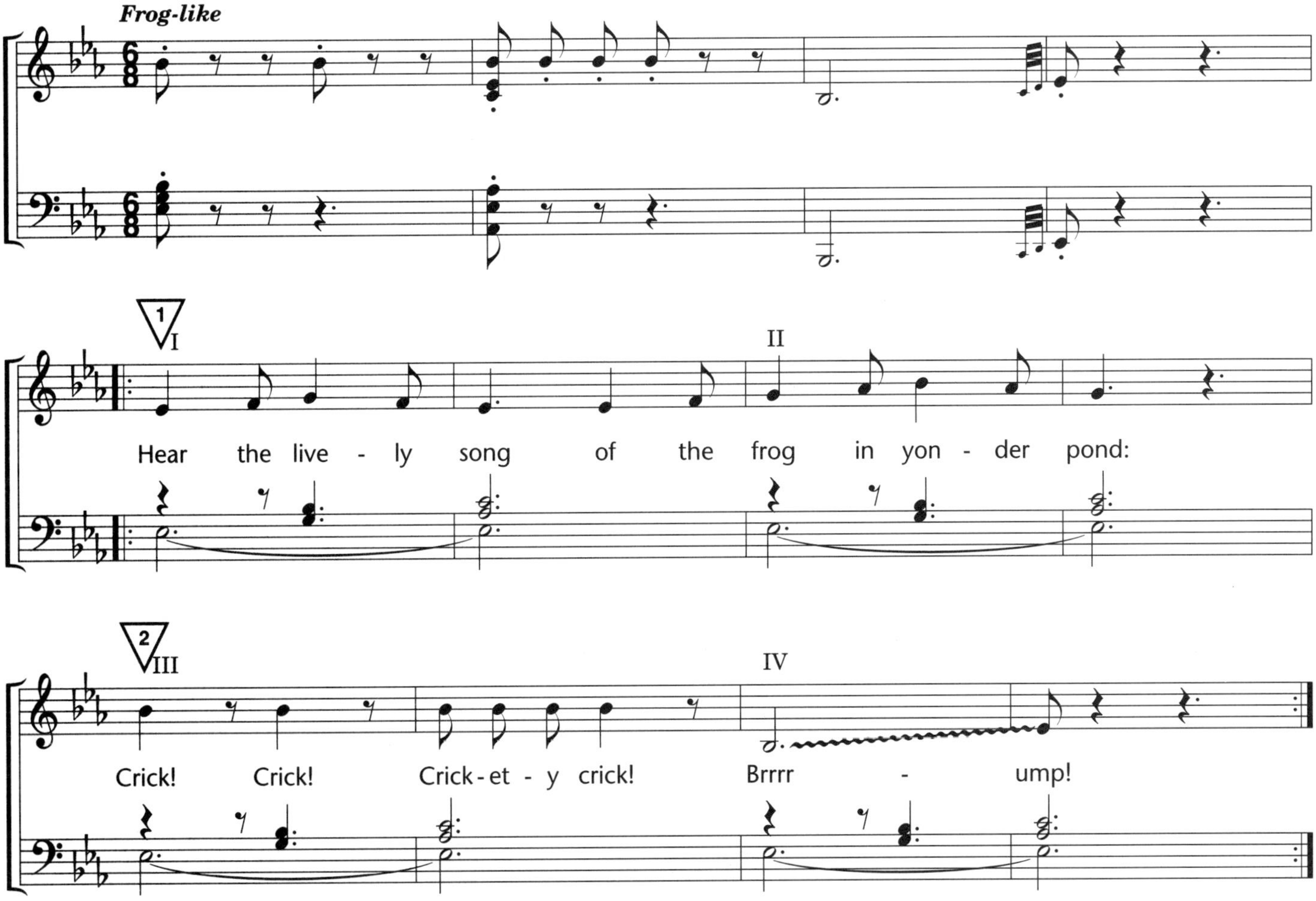

Student Page 231

Los niños en España cantan (In Spain the Children Sing)

English Words by S. T.

Folk Song from Mexico
Arranged by Christopher Hatcher

Student Page 232

Let Music Surround You

Words and Music by Fran Smartt Addicott
Arranged by Christopher Hatcher

The Keel Row

Folk Song from Northumbria
Arranged by John Pivarnik

4. The rooster ran off and the oxen all died,
   The last piece of bacon that morning was fried.
   Poor Ike got discouraged and Betsy got mad,
   The dog wagged his tail and looked awfully sad. *Refrain*

5. The alkali desert was burning and hot,
   And Ike, he decided to leave on the spot:
   "My dear old Pike County, I'll go back to you."
   Said Betsy, "You'll go by yourself if you do." *Refrain*

6. They swam the wide rivers, they crossed the tall peaks,
   They camped out on prairies for weeks and for weeks,
   Fought hunger and rattlers and big storms of dust,
   Determined to reach California or bust. *Refrain*

Student Page 244

Theme from New York, New York

Words by Fred Ebb
Music by John Kander
Arranged by John Girt

Blow, Ye Winds

Folk Song from the United States
Arranged by Benjamin Carter

3. It's now we're out to sea, my boys, the wind begins to blow,
   One half the watch is sick on deck and the other half below. *Refrain*

4. The skipper's on the quarter-deck, a-squinting at the sails,
   When up aloft the look-out sights a school of whales. *Refrain*

5. "Now clear away the boats, my boys, and after him we'll trail,
   But if you get too near to him, he'll kick you with his tail!" *Refrain*

6. Now we've got him turned up, we tow him alongside;
   We over with our blubber hooks and rob him of his hide. *Refrain*

7. Next comes the stowing down, my boys; 'twill take both night and day,
   And you'll all have fifty cents apiece when you collect your pay. *Refrain*

Rio Grande

Shantey from the United States
Arranged by Darrell Peter

3. The anchor's aweigh and the sails they are set, . . .
   The gals that we're leaving we'll never forget, . . .   *Refrain*

4. Goodbye to Sally and Sarah and Sue, . . .
   To all who are list'ning, it's goodbye to you, . . .   *Refrain*

sounds an ech - o__ in my soul, how can I keep from sing - ing?__
love is lord of__ heaven and earth, how can I keep from sing - ing?__
friends by shame are__ un - de - filed, how can I keep from sing - ing?__

Student Page 254

The Glendy Burke

Words and Music by Stephen Foster
Arranged by Ting Ho

Bouncy
VERSE

1. The Glen - dy Burke is a might - y fast boat, With a might - y fast cap - tain
2. The Glen - dy Burke has a fun - ny old crew, And they sing__ the boat - man's

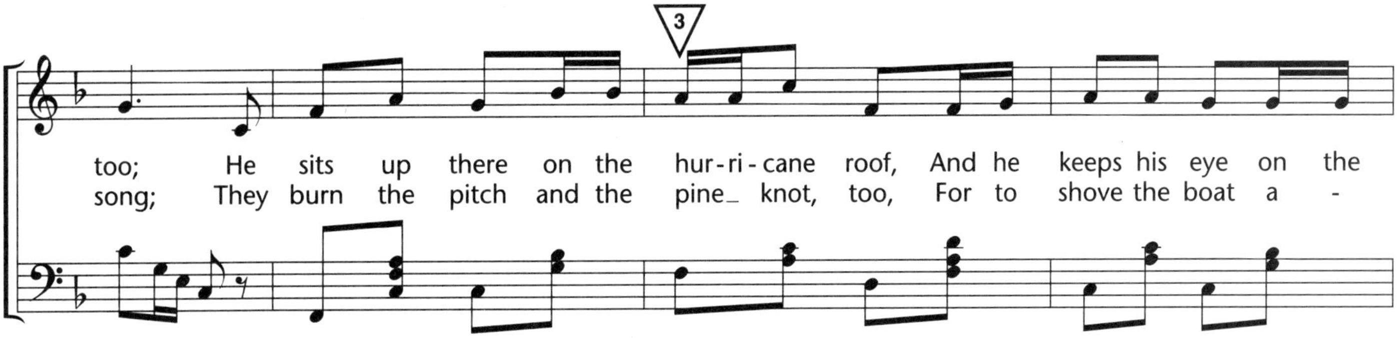

too; He sits up there on the hur - ri - cane roof, And he keeps his eye on the
song; They burn the pitch and the pine_ knot, too, For to shove the boat a -

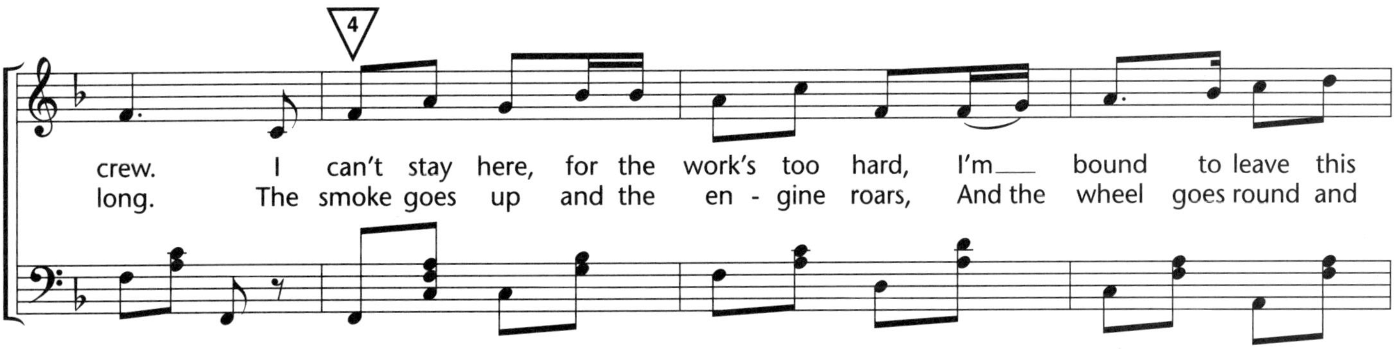

crew. I can't stay here, for the work's too hard, I'm__ bound to leave this
long. The smoke goes up and the en - gine roars, And the wheel goes round and

Student Page 256

Oh, Susanna

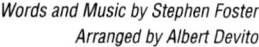
Words and Music by Stephen Foster
Arranged by Albert Devito

2. Now the riverbank will make a mighty good road;
   Dead trees will show you the way.
   And the left foot, pegfoot, travelin' on,
   Just you follow the drinkin' gourd.

Student Page 260

Cielito lindo

English Words by Alice Firgau

Folk Song from Mexico
Arranged by Wallace Schmidt

1. De la sierra morena, Cielito lindo, vienen ba-
1. From the dark, distant mountain, Cielito lindo, I see de-

jando, Un par de ojitos negros, Cielito
scending, Your dark eyes flashing brightly, Cielito

lindo, de contrabando. Ay, ay, ay, ay!
lindo, love's message sending. Ay, ay, ay, ay!

Canta y no llores. Porque cantando se a-
Sing, sing with gladness. For in those hearts that are

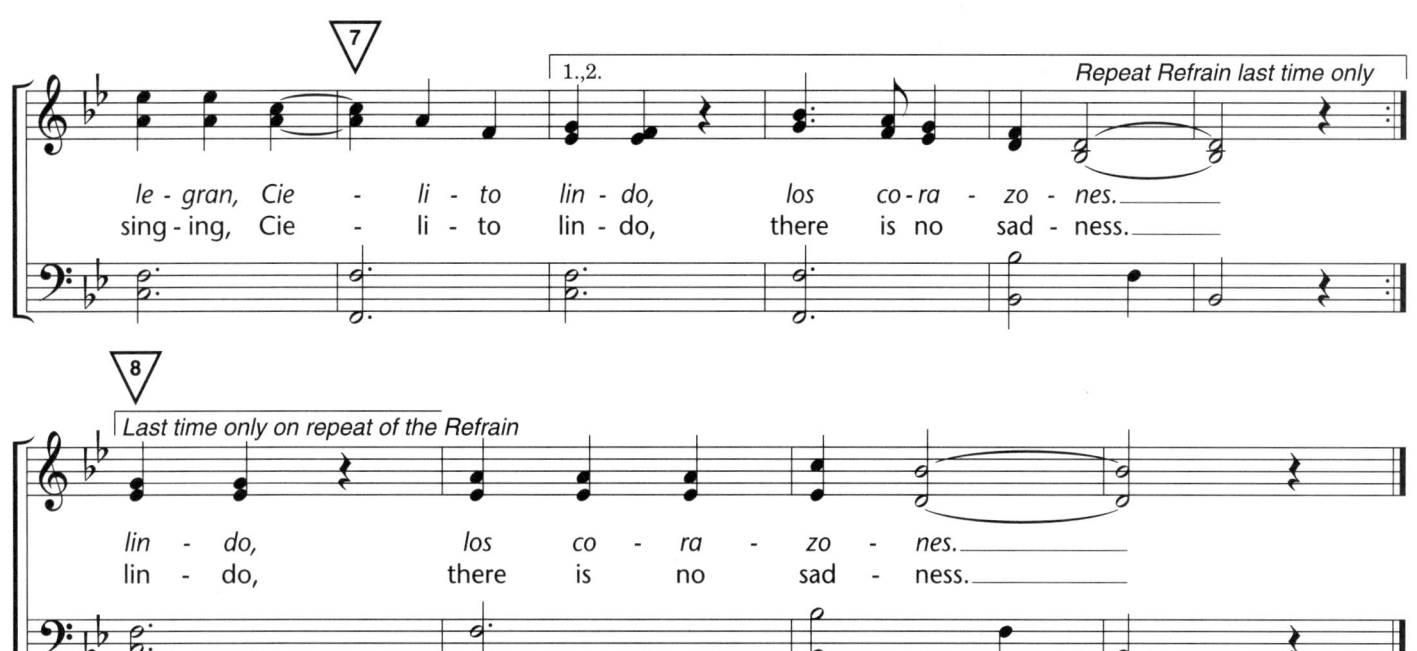

2. *Ese lunar que tienes, Cielito lindo,*
   Junto a la boca,
   No se lo des a nadie, Cielito lindo,
   que a mi me toca. Refrain

2. For your kisses, my lovely Cielito lindo,
   My heart is aching.
   And when I can't be near you, Cielito lindo,
   my heart is breaking. *Refrain*

Streets of Laredo

Cowboy Song from the United States
Arranged by Edward Paynter

//
//
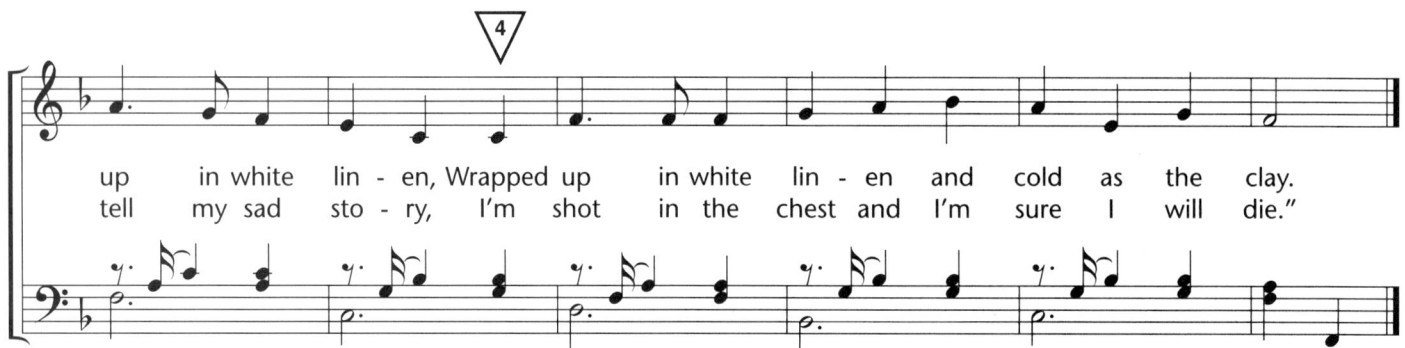

1. As I walked out in the streets of Laredo, As I walked out in Laredo one day, I spied a young cowboy wrapped up in white linen, Wrapped up in white linen and cold as the clay.

2. "I see by your outfit that you are a cowboy," These words he said as I boldly walked by. "Come listen to me and I'll tell my sad story, I'm shot in the chest and I'm sure I will die."

3. "Now once in the saddle I used to ride handsome, 'A handsome young cowboy' is what they would say. I'd ride into town and go down to the cardhouse, But I'm shot in the chest and I'm dying today."

4. "Go run to the spring for a cup of cold water, To cool down my fever," the young cowboy said. But when I returned, his poor soul had departed, And I wept when I saw the young cowboy was dead.

5. We'll bang the drum slowly and play the fife lowly, We'll play the dead march as we bear him along. We'll go to the graveyard and lay the sod o'er him; He was a young cowboy, but he had done wrong.

Route 66

Words and Music by Bobby Troup
Arranged by Buddy Skipper

California, Here I Come

Words and Music by Al Jolson, Bud DeSylva, and Joseph Meyer
Arranged by Joyce Kalbach

Pastures of Plenty

Words and Music by Woody Guthrie
Arranged by Alice Firgau

TRO © Copyright 1960 (Renewed) 1963 (Renewed) Ludlow Music, Inc., New York, New York. Used by permission.

deserts was hot and your mountains was cold.
come with the dust and we're gone with the wind.
work in this fight, and we'll fight 'till we win.
pastures of plenty must always be free.

Student Page 278

Cotton-Eye Joe

Folk Song from Tennessee
Arranged by Martin Quarles

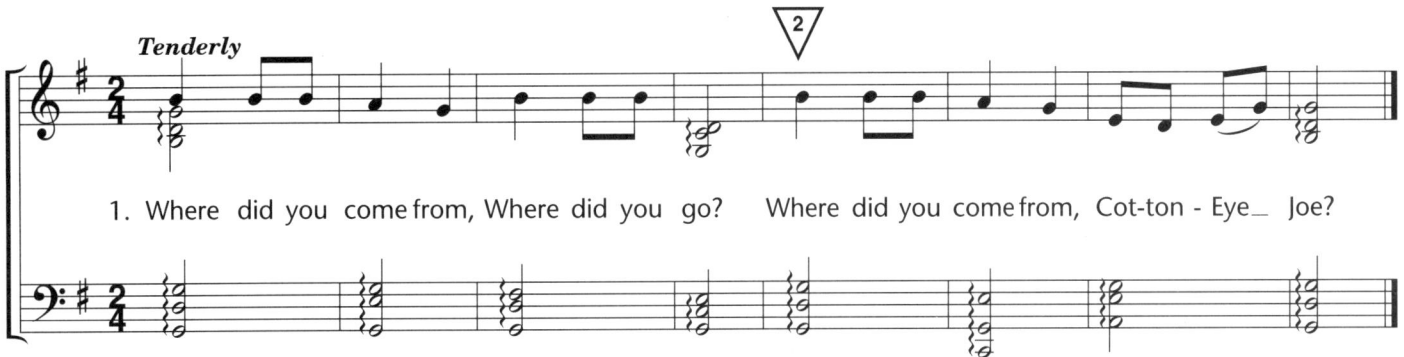

1. Where did you come from, Where did you go? Where did you come from, Cotton-Eye Joe?

2. I've come for to see you,
   I've come for to sing,
   I've come for to bring you
   A song and a ring.

3. When did you leave here?
   Where did you go?
   When you comin' back here,
   Cotton-Eye Joe?

4. Left here last winter,
   I've wandered through the year.
   Seen people dyin',
   Seen them with their fear.

5. I've been to the cities,
   Buildings cracking down,
   Seen the people calling,
   Falling to the ground.

6. I'll come back tomorrow,
   If I can find a ride,
   Or I'll sail in the breezes,
   Blowin' on the tide.

7. Well, when you do come back here,
   Look what I have brung,
   A meadow to be run in,
   A song to be sung.

8. Where did you come from?
   Where did you go?
   Where did you come from,
   Cotton-Eye Joe?

Ai Dunaiĭ moy (Ah, My Merry Dunaii)

English Words by Charles Haywood

Folk Song from Russia
Arranged by Paul Somers

Beriozka (The Birch Tree)

Folk Song from Russia
Arranged by Paul Beck

2. Oh, my little tree, I need branches,
   For three silver flutes I need three branches,
   Loo-lee-loo, three branches,
   Loo-lee-loo, three branches.

3. From another branch I will make now,
   I will make a tingling balalaika,
   Loo-lee-loo, balalaika,
   Loo-lee-loo, balalaika.

4. When I play my new balalaika,
   I will think of you, my lovely birch tree,
   Loo-lee-loo, lovely birch tree,
   Loo-lee-loo, lovely birch tree.

The Bard of Armagh

Words attributed to Thomas Campbell

Folk Tune from Ireland
Arranged by Rory Boyle

Student Page 290

Tina singu

Folk Song from South Africa
Arranged by Ting Ho and Don Kalbach

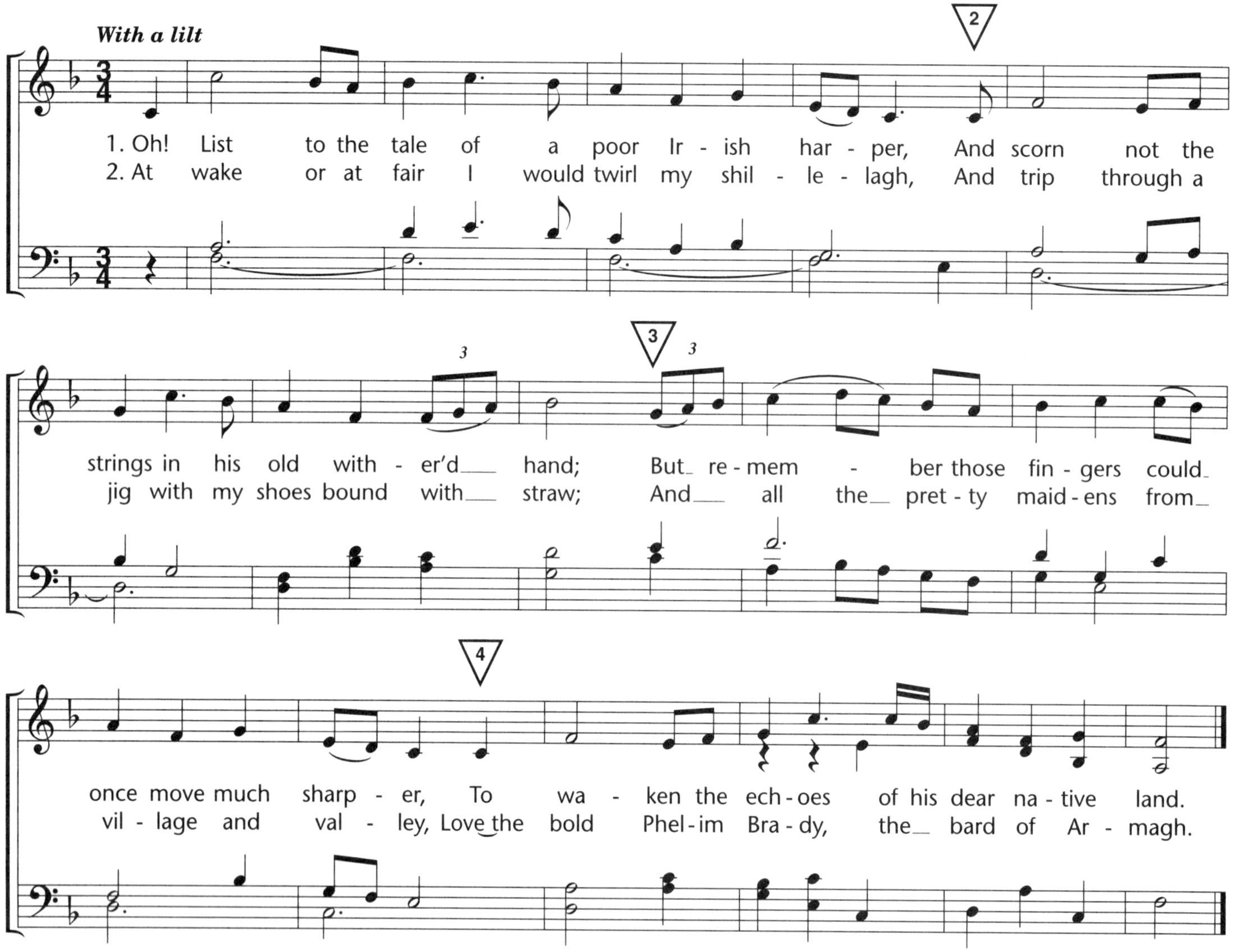

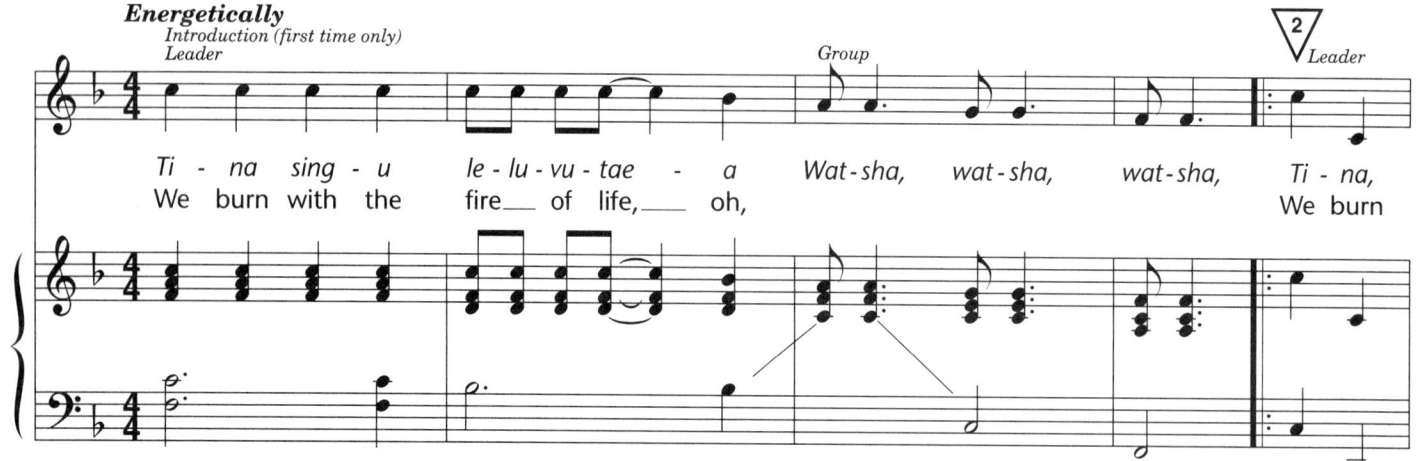

La raspa

English Words by Kim Williams

Folk Song from Mexico
Arranged by Joyce Kalbach

Gracefully

La ras - pa yo bai - lé al de - re - cho y al re - vés. Si
The ras - pa I will dance, as for - ward and back I go. So

quie - res tú bai - lar, em - pie - za a mo - ver los pies.
if you want to dance, be - gin with your heel and toe.

Brin - ca, brin - ca, brin - ca tam - bién, mue - ve, mue - ve mu - cho los pies. Que la
Al - ways mov - ing, mov - ing your feet, back and forth now jump to the beat. This is

ras - pa vas a bai - lar al de - re - cho y al re - vés.
how the dance we will do, laugh - ing, laugh - ing all the way through.

Si quie - res tú bai - lar la ras - pa co - mo yo, Me
So if you want to dance the ras - pa the way I do, Be -

Student Page 296

Sakura

English Version by Lorene Hoyt

Folk Song from Japan
Modern Arrangement by Henry Burnett
Arranged by S. Hagiwara

Moderately

Sa - ku - ra, Sa - ku - ra, Ya - yo - i no so - ra__ wa,
1. Sa - ku - ra, Sa - ku - ra, Cher - ry blos - soms ev - 'ry - where.
2. Sa - ku - ra, Sa - ku - ra, Blos - soms wav - ing in the__ breeze.

Mi - wa - ta - su ka - gi - ri, Ka - su - mi ka ku - mo - ka,
Clouds of glo - ry fill the__ sky, Mist of beau - ty in the__ air,
Yo - shi - no, the cher - ry__ land, Tat - su - ta, the ma - ple__ trees,

Ni - o - i zo i - zu - ru; I - za - ya, i - za - ya
Love - ly col - ors float - ing__ by, Sa - ku - ra, Sa - ku - ra,
Ka - ra - sa - ki, pine tree__ grand, Sa - ku - ra, Sa - ku - ra,

Mi____ ni yu - kan._____
Let____ all come____ sing - ing.
Let____ all come____ sing - ing.

148

Shri Ram, jai Ram

Hindu Chant
Arranged by Ian MacDonald

Feng yang hua gu (Feng Yang Song)

Folk Song from China

Xiao (Bamboo Flute)

Folk Song from China
Arranged by John Detroy

Student Page 304

Yibane amenu

Round from Israel
Arranged by Georgette LeNorth

Student Page 310

Love Will Guide Us

Words by Sally Rogers

Traditional Melody
Arranged by Mark A. Miller

Liltingly

Refrain: Love will guide us, peace had tried us.
1. If you cannot sing like angels,

Hope inside us will lead the way,
If you cannot speak before thousands,

On the road from greed to giving.
You can give from deep within you.

Love will guide us through the dark night. *(to Verses)*
You can change the world with your love. *(to Refrain)*

2. You are like no other being.
   What you can give, no other can give,
   To the future of our precious children.
   To the future of the world where we live.
   (to Refrain)

3. Hear the song of peace within you.
   Heed the song of peace in your heart.
   Spring's new beginning shall lead to the harvest.
   Love will guide us on our way.
   (to Refrain)

Student Page 318

Big Rock Candy Mountain

Traditional
Arranged by Billy Joe Lafayette

Brightly

1. In the Big Rock Candy Mountain There's a land that's fair and bright,
   Where the hand-outs grow on bushes, And you sleep out ev'ry night;
   Where the box-cars all are emp-ty, And the sun shines ev'ry
2. In the Big Rock Candy Mountain Where the ho-bo nev-er begs,
   And the bull-dogs all are tooth-less, And the hens lay soft-boiled eggs;
   All the trees are full of ap-ples, And the barns are full of

Niu lang zhi nü (The Cowherd and the Weaving Maid)

English Words by Mary Shamrock
Folk Song from China
Arranged by Ting Ho

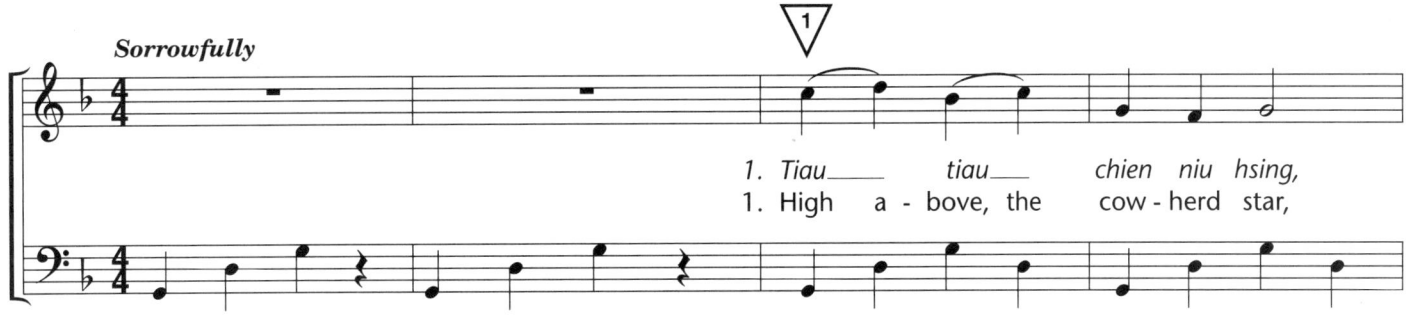

2. Zhong zhru bu cheng zhang,
   chi ti lei zhru ü
   ne han ching chie chien
   hsiang chü fu ji hsü
   ing ing i hsuei jien
   muo muo bu de ü

2. They must wait throughout the day
   for the moon to light the way.
   Each alone, through the years
   freely flow the tears.
   Shining far apart,
   weeping with a silent heart.

My Bonnie Lies Over the Ocean

Folk Song from the United States
Arranged by Neil Swanson

With feeling

VERSE

1. My Bonnie lies over the ocean, My Bonnie lies over the sea; My Bonnie lies over the ocean, Oh, bring back my Bonnie to me.
2. Last night as I lay on my pillow, last night as I lay on my bed; Last night as I lay on my pillow, I dreamt that my Bonnie was dead.
3. Oh, blow ye winds over the ocean, Oh blow ye winds over the sea; Oh, blow ye winds over the ocean, And bring back my Bonnie to me.
4. The winds have blown over the ocean, The winds have blown over the sea; The winds have blown over the ocean, And brought back my Bonnie to me.

REFRAIN

Bring back, bring back, Bring back my Bonnie to me, to me; Bring back, bring back, Oh, bring back my Bonnie to me.

Student Page 329

Clementine

Folk Song from the United States
Arranged by W. W. Schmidt

1. In a cavern by a canyon, Excavating for a mine, Dwelt a miner, forty-niner, And his daughter, Clementine.
2. Light she was and like a feather, And her shoes were number nine, Herring boxes without topses, Sandals were for Clementine.

REFRAIN
Oh, my darlin', oh, my darlin', Oh, my darlin' Clementine, You are lost and gone forever, Dreadful sorry, Clementine.

3. Drove she ducklings to the water
   Every morning just at nine;
   Struck her foot against a splinter,
   Fell into the foaming brine. *Refrain*

4. Rosy lips above the water
   Blowing bubbles mighty fine;
   But, alas! I was no swimmer,
   So I lost my Clementine. *Refrain*

Student Page 336

Peace Round

Traditional
Arranged by Neil Swanson

Somos el barco (We Are the Boat)

Words and Music by Lorre Wyatt
Arranged by Anita P. Davis

Student Page 343

This Pretty Planet

Words and Music by John Forster and Tom Chapin
Arranged by Mary Jean Nelson

174

For the Beauty of the Earth

Words by Folliott S. Pierpoint
Music by Conrad Kocher

3. For the joy of ear and eye,
   For the heart and mind's delight,
   For the mystic harmony
   Linking sense to sound and sight.
   Lord of all, to Thee we raise
   This our hymn of grateful praise.

4. For the joy of human love,
   Brother, sister, parent, child,
   Friends on earth and friends above,
   For all gentle thoughts and mild.
   Lord of all, to Thee we raise
   This our hymn of grateful praise.

Singin' in the Rain

Words by Arthur Freed

Music by Nacio Herb Brown
Arrangement by Cheryl Terhune Cronk

Cheerfully

I'm sing - in' in the rain, just sing - in' in the rain. What a glo - ri - ous feel - ing, I'm hap - py a - gain! I'm laugh - ing at clouds so dark up a - bove. The sun's___ in my heart___ and I'm

simile

Student Page 350

The Wheel of the Water

Words and Music by John Forster and Tom Chapin
Arranged by Don Kalbach

Cycle Song of Life (The River Song)

Words and music by James Durst
Arranged by Neil Swanson

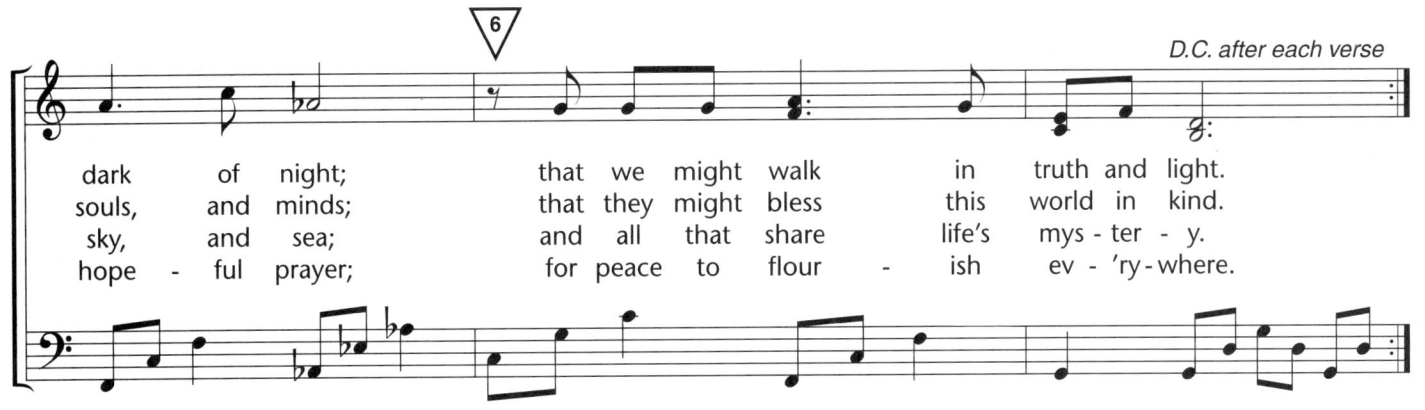

D.C. after each verse

dark of night; that we might walk in truth and light.
souls, and minds; that they might bless this world in kind.
sky, and sea; and all that share life's mys-ter-y.
hope-ful prayer; for peace to flour-ish ev-'ry-where.

Student Page 362

Sailboat in the Sky

English Words by Aura Kontra

Folk Song from Korea
Arranged by John Detroy

Smoothly

Pu reun ha nul eun-ha su ha yan jjok bae
See the small white boat in the sky, sail-ing toward the

ae, Gae su na mu han-na mu
west, High a-bove the cin-na-mon tree

to kki han ma ri, Dot dae do ah
where a rab-bit rests. With no sails or

183

ni dal go sat dae do up si, Ga gi do
oars, it skims o'er the Mil-ky Way, Float-ing a-

jal do gahn da so- jjok na ra ro.
mong the clouds as slow-ly it fades a- way.

Student Page 366

Shake the Papaya Down

Calypso Song
Arranged by Ruth E. Dwyer and Judith M. Waller
Edited by Henry H. Leck
Piano Arrangement by John Girt

Exuberantly

Ma - ma says no play;
Sweet, sweet pa - pa - ya,

184

Student Page 371

Lullaby and Dance

Traditional
Arranged by Ruth E. Dwyer
Piano Arrangement by Carol Jay

Student Page 375

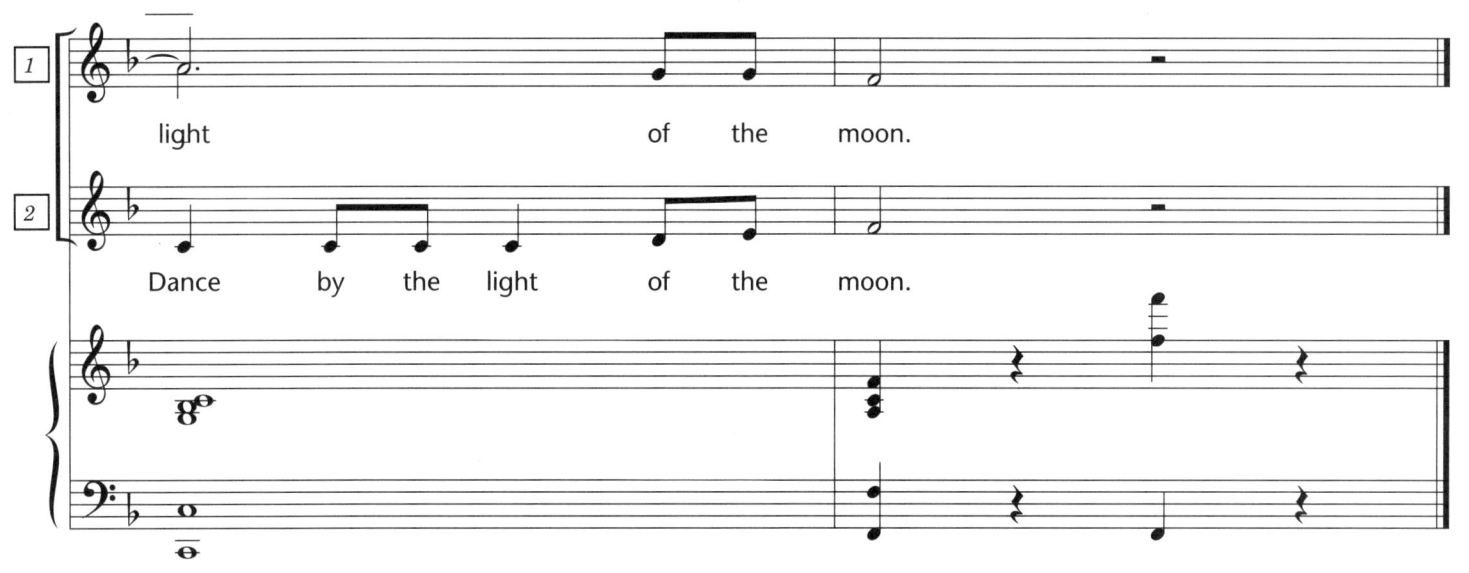

Einini

Gaelic Folk Song
Arranged by Cyndee Giebler
Piano Arrangment by Carol Jay

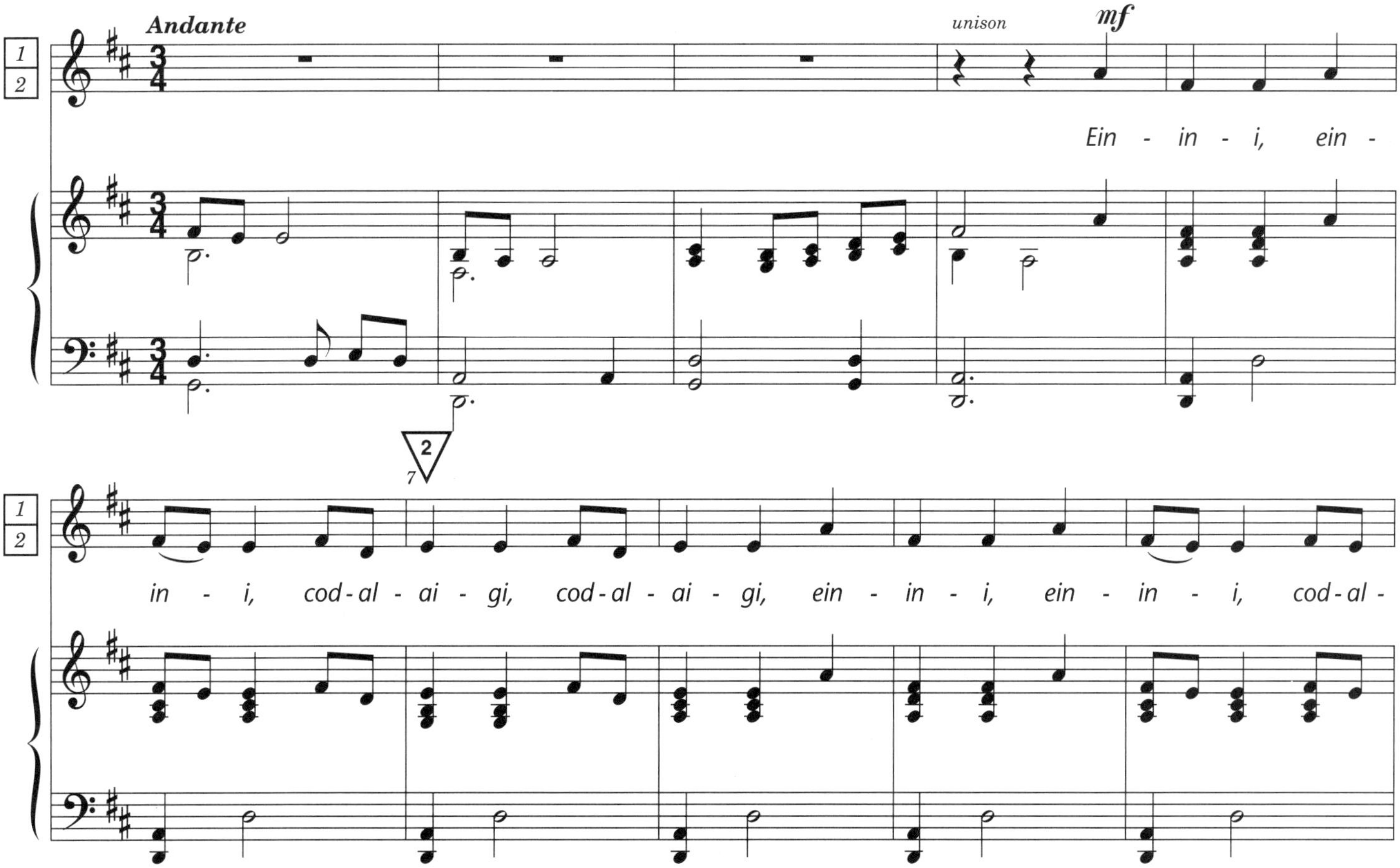

Student Page 378

Little David, Play on Your Harp

African American Spiritual
Arranged by Linda Williams

Circle 'Round the Moon from "Reflections of Youth"

Words and Music by Mark Hierholzer

Student Page 395

A Merry Modal Christmas

Words and Music by Bernard de la Monnoye (Pat-a-Pan)
Carols from France and England
Arranged by Buryl Red

214

Student Page 398

La copa de la vida (The Cup of Life)

Words and Music by Desmond Child and Robi Rosa
Arranged by Buddy Skipper

Shir l'shalom (Hand in Hand — A Song for Peace)

Hebrew Words by Jacob Rotblitt
English Adaptation by Stanley Ralph Ross and Michael Isaacson
Music by Yair Rosenblum
Arranged by David Eddleman

Little Shop of Horrors

Words by Howard Ashman
Music by Alan Menken
Arranged by Buddy Skipper

Let It Snow! Let It Snow! Let It Snow!

Word by Sammy Cahn

Music by Jule Styne
Arranged by John Girt

Festive

VERSE

The snow-man in the yard is fro-zen hard; He's a sor-ry sight to see,

If he had a brain he'd com-plain, Bet he wish-es he were me.

REFRAIN

Oh! the weath-er out-side is fright-ful, but the fire is so de-light-ful. And since we've no place to go, Let it snow! Let it snow! Let it snow!

It does-n't show signs of stop-ping, and I brought some corn for pop-ping; The lights are turned way down low. Let it snow! Let it snow! Let it snow!

Ocho kandelikas (Eight Little Candles)

Words and Music by Flory Jagoda
Arranged by Ting Ho

3. Los pastelikos vo komer
   kon almendrikas i la myel.
   Los pastelikos vo komer
   kon almendrikas i la myel.
   Refrain

3. Sweet little pastries we will eat,
   filled with almonds and honey.
   Sweet little pastries we will eat,
   filled with almonds and honey.
   Refrain

The Twelve Days of Christmas

Christmas Song from England
Arranged by James Harris

Harambee

Words and Music by James McBride
Arranged by Joseph Joubert

Dayenu (It Would Have Been Enough)

Jewish Passover Song
Arranged by David ben Avraham

Happily

VERSE

1. I - lu ho - tzi, ho - tzi - a - nu, ho - tzi - a - nu mi - Mitz - ra - yim,
2. I - lu na - tan na - tan la - nu, na - tan la - nu et ha - Sha - bat,
1. Had he led us out of E - gypt, on - ly led us out of E - gypt,
2. Had he giv - en us the Sab - bath, on - ly giv - en us the Sab - bath,

ho - tzi - a - nu mi - Mitz - ra - yim, da - ye - nu.
na - tan la - nu et ha - Sha - bat, da - ye - nu.
Had he led us out of E - gypt, da - ye - nu.
Had he giv - en us the Sab - bath, da - ye - nu.

Da - da - ye - nu, da - da - ye - nu, da - da - ye - nu, da -

ye - nu, da - ye - nu, da - ye - nu. ye - nu, da - ye - nu!

3. Ilu natan natan lanu,
natan lanu et haTora,
natan lanu et haTora, dayenu.
Refrain

3. Had he given us the Tora,
only given us the Tora,
Had he given us the Tora, *dayenu*.
Refrain

Student Page 424

America

Words by Samuel Francis Smith
Traditional Melody

1. My country! 'tis of thee, Sweet land of liberty, Of thee I sing; Land where my fathers died, Land of the Pilgrims' pride, From ev'ry mountainside, Let freedom ring!

2. My native country, thee, Land of the noble free, Thy name I love; I love thy rocks and rills, Thy woods and templed hills; My heart with rapture thrills Like that above.

3. Let music swell the breeze,
   And ring from all the trees
   Sweet Freedom's song;
   Let mortal tongues awake,
   Let all that breathe partake,
   Let rocks their silence break,
   The sound prolong.

4. Our fathers' God, to Thee,
   Author of liberty,
   To Thee we sing;
   Long may our land be bright
   With Freedom's holy light;
   Protect us by Thy might,
   Great God, our King!

CREDITS AND ACKNOWLEDGMENTS *continued*

(Continued from page 2)

International), Kentucky Sweetheart Music, and Inspector Barlow Music. All Rights Reserved. International Copyright Secured. Used by Permission. 160: "We Shall Overcome" musical and lyrical adaptation by Zilphia Horton, Frank Hamilton, Guy Carawan and Pete Seeger. Inspired by African American Gospel Singing, members of the Food & Tobacco Workers Union, Charleston, SC and the southern Civil Rights Movement. TRO–© 1960 (Renewed) and 1963 (Renewed) Ludlow Music, Inc., New York, International Copyright Secured. Made in U.S.A. All rights reserved including Public Performance for Profit. Royalties derived from this composition are being contributed to the We Shall Overcome Fund and The Freedom Movement under the Trusteeship of the writers. Used by permission. 161: "Love Will Guide Us" Lyrics © 1985 Sally Rogers, (p) Thrushwood Press Pub., BMI. Tune: "I Will Guide Thee" (PD). Reprinted by permission. 162: "Big Rock Candy Mountain" © 2002 Pearson Education, Inc. 164: "Sailing Down My Golden River" Words and music by Pete Seeger. TRO–© Copyright 1971 (Renewed) Melody Trails, Inc., New York, NY. Used by permission. 165: "Niu lang zhi nü" (The Cowherd and the Weaving Maid) English words © 1998 Silver Burdett Ginn. 168: "Johnny Appleseed" by Stephen Vincent Benet, from *A Book of Americans* by Rosemary and Stephen Vincent Benet. Copyright © 1933 by Rosemary and Stephen Vincent Benet. Copyright renewed © 1961 by Rosemary Carr Benet. Reprinted by permission of Brandt and Brandt Literary Agents, Inc. 169: "Peace Round" by Jean Ritchie. © 1964, 1977 Jean Ritchie, Geordie Music Publishing Co. Reprinted with permission. 170: "Somos el barco" (We Are the Boat) by Lorre Wyatt, Judith Cook Tucker, and Bill Vanaverr, *Roots & Branches Music*. 174: "This Pretty Planet" Words and music by John Forster and Tom Chapin. Copyright © 1988 The Last Music Company (ASCAP) /Limousine Music Co. (ASCAP) This arrangement © 1989 The Last Music Company/Limousine Music Co. Reprinted by permission. 176: "Singin' In The Rain" by Nacio Herb Brown and Arthur Freed. © 1929 (Renewed) Metro-Goldwyn-Mayer Inc. All Rights controlled by EMI Robbins Catalog Inc. All Rights Reserved. Used by Permission. WARNER BROS. PUBLICATIONS U.S. INC., Miami, FL 33014. 178: "The Wheel of Water" Words and music by John Forster and Tom Chapin. © 1990 Limousine Music Co. & The Last Music Co. (ASCAP) Reprinted by permission. 179: "Cycle Song of Life (The River Song)" By James Durst. Copyright © 1974, 1997, PhoeniXongs ASCAP. Reprinted with permission. 182: "Starlight, Star Bright" by James Durst. Copyright © 1993 PhoeniXongs ASCAP. Reprinted with permission. 183: "Sailboat in the Sky" English words © 1995 Silver Burdett Ginn. 184: "Shake the Papaya Down" Calypso Song arranged by Ruth E. Dwyer and Judith M. Waller, edited by Henry H. Leck. Copyright Transferred 2000, Colla Voce Music, Inc. 4600 Sunset Avenue, #83, Indianapolis, IN 46208. Reprinted by permission of Colla Voce Music, Inc. 192: "Lullaby and Dance" by Ruth E. Dwyer. 197: "Einini" (Gaelic Folk Song) arranged by Cyndee Geibler. 201: "Little David, Play on Your Harp" Arrangement © 2002 Pearson Education, Inc. 202: "Sambalele" © 2002 Pearson Education, Inc. 208: "Circle Round the Moon" Words and music by Mark Hierholzer. 214: "A Merry Modal Christmas" Arrangement © 2002 Pearson Education, Inc. 222: "La copa de la vida," (The Cup of Life) English lyrics by Robi Rosa and Desmond Child. Spanish lyrics by Luis Gomez Escolar. © 1998, 1999 A Phantom Vox Publishing, Universal-Polygram International Publishing, Inc., Desmophobis and Musica Calaca, S.L. All Rights for A Phantom Vox Publishing administered by Warner-Tamerlane Publishing Corp. All Rights Reserved. Used by Permission. WARNER BROS. PUBLICATIONS U.S. INC., Miami, FL 33014. 228: "Shir L'Shalom" (Hand in Hand–A Song for Peace) Last Song of Yitzchak Rabin. Music and words by Yair Rosenblum, arranged by Michael Isaacson. Used by permission Transcontinental Music Publications. 633 Third Avenue. NY, NY 10017. 231: "Little Shop of Horrors" Words by Howard Ashman, music by Alan Menken. © 1982 Trunksong Music, Ltd. (BMI) Menken Music (BMI), & MCA-Geffen Music (ASCAP). All Rights o/b/o Trunksong Music Ltd. administered by Warner-Tamerlane Publishing Corp. (BMI). All Rights Reserved. Used by Permission. WARNER BROS. PUBLICATIONS U.S. INC., Miami, FL 33014. 235: "Al quebrar la piñata" (Piñata Song) English words © 1988 Silver Burdett Ginn. 236: "Winter Fantasy" Words and music by Jill Gallina. Copyright © 1982 by Shawnee Press, Inc. (ASCAP). International Copyright Secured. All Rights Reserved. 238: "Let It Snow, Let It Snow, Let It Snow," by Sammy Cahn and Jule Styne. © 1945 Cahn Music Company. © Renewed, assigned to Cahn Music Company & Producers Music Pub. Co., Inc. All Rights o/b/o Cahn Music Company administered by WB Music Corp. All rights c/b/o Producers Music Pub. Co., Inc. administered by Chappell & Co. All Rights Reserved. Used by Permission. WARNER BROS. PUBLICATIONS U.S. INC., Miami, FL 33014 240: "Ocho kandelikas"(Eight Little Candles) Words and music by Flory Jagoda from *The Flory Jagoda Songbook* 1993. Reprinted with permission of the author. 246: "Harambee" © 1995 Silver Burdett Ginn.

The editors of Scott, Foresman and Company have made every attempt to verify the source of "Gakavik (The Partridge)" (p. 14), "Son Macarón" (p. 61), "Canción de cuna" (p. 75), "Dry Bones Come Skipping" (p. 111), and "Thula, thula, ngoana (Sleep, Sleep, Baby)" (p. 113), but were unable to do so. We believe them to be in the public domain. Every effort has been made to locate all the copyright holders of material used in this book. If any errors or omissions have occurred, corrections will be made.

Song Index

Ah, My Merry Dunaiĭ (*Ai Dunaii moy*) 142
Ah, Poor Bird 97
Ai Dunaiĭ moy (Ah, My Merry Dunaii) 142
Ala Da'lona 73
Al quebrar la piñata (Piñata Song) 235
All Night, All Day 95
Amazing Grace 81
America 251
America, the Beautiful 82
At the Hop 87

Bamboo Flute (*Xiao*) 152
Bard of Armagh, The 144
Beriozka (The Birch Tree) 143
Big Ranch, The (*El rancho grande*) 108
Big Rock Candy Mountain 162
Birch Tree, The (*Beriozka*) 143
Biting Wind (*Ōsamu kosamu*) 54
Blow Ye Winds 124
Bluebells (*Doraji*) 92

California, Here I Come 139
Canción de cuna (Cradle Song) 75
Canoe Song 52
Cantando mentiras (Singing Tall Tales) 78
Chairs to Mend 79
Cielito lindo 132
Circle 'Round the Moon 208
Clementine 167
Computer, The 98
Cotton-Eye Joe 141
Cowherd and the Weaving Maid, The (*Niu lang zhi nü*) 165
Cradle Song (*Canción de cuna*) 75
Cumberland Gap 74
Cup of Life, The (*La copa de la vida*) 222
Cycle Song of Life 179

Dancing (*Tancovačka*) 114
Dayenu (It Would Have Been Enough) 250
Doraji (Bluebells) 92
Do Wah Diddy Diddy 100
Dry Bones 84
Dry Bones Come Skipping 111

Eh, cumpari! (Hey, Buddy!) 45
Eight Little Candles (*Ocho kandelikas*) 240
Einini 197
El rancho grande (The Big Ranch) 108

Feng yang hua gu (Feng Yang Song) 150
Feng Yang Song (*Feng yang hua gu*) 150
Follow the Drinkin' Gourd 130
For the Beauty of the Earth 175
Freedom from *Shenandoah* 106
Frog Music 99
Frog Round 115

Gakavik (The Partridge) 14
Glendy Burke, The 127
Going 'Round (*Hashewie*) 41
Gonna Ride Up in the Chariot 17

Hand in Hand–A Song for Peace (*Shir l'shalom*) 228
Happy Wanderer, The 50
Harambee 246
Hashewie (Going 'Round) 41
Haul Away, Joe 13
Hey, Buddy! (*Eh, cumpari!*) 45
Hey, m'tswala 52
How Can I Keep from Singing? 126

I Believe I Can Fly 101
I'm Gonna Sing 24
In Spain the Children Sing (*Los niños en España cantan*) 116
It Would Have Been Enough (*Dayenu*) 250

Joe Turner Blues 37
Johnny Appleseed 168

Keel Row, The 117
Kookaburra 96

La copa de la vida (The Cup of Life) 222
La raspa 146
La Tarara 93
Let It Snow! Let It Snow! Let It Snow! 238
Let Music Surround You 116
Liebe ist ein Ring (Love Is Like a Ring) 98
Limbo Like Me 16
Lion Sleeps Tonight, The 72
Little David, Play on Your Harp 201
Little Shop of Horrors 231
Los niños en España cantan (In Spain the Children Sing) 116
Love Can Build a Bridge 156
Love Is Like a Ring (*Liebe ist ein Ring*) 98
Love Will Guide Us 161
Lullaby and Dance 192

Merry Modal Christmas, A 214
Minka 112
Missy-La, Massa-La 96
Moon, The (*Tsuki*) 15
My Bonnie Lies Over the Ocean 166
My Home's Across the Blue Ridge Mountains 48

Niu lang zhi nü (The Cowherd and the Weaving Maid) 165

Ochimbo 66
Ocho kandelikas (Eight Little Candles) 240
Ode to Joy 80
Oh, Danny Boy 34
Oh, How Lovely Is the Evening 110
Oh, Susanna 128
Old House, Tear It Down! 94
Ōsamu kosamu (Biting Wind) 54
Over My Head 64
Over the Rainbow 76

Partridge, The (*Gakavik*) 14
Pastures of Plenty 140
Paw-Paw Patch 53
Pay Me My Money Down 25
Peace Round 169
Piñata Song (*Al quebrar la piñata*) 235
Put a Little Love in Your Heart 10

Rio Grande 125
Riquirrán 42
Rise and Shine 56
River 38
Rock Island Line 36
Route 66 135

Sailboat in the Sky 183
Sailing Down My Golden River 164
Sakura 148
Sambalele 202
Santa Clara 90
See the Children Playin' 60
Shake the Papaya Down 184
Shir l'shalom (Hand in Hand–A Song for Peace) 228
Shri Ram, jai Ram 149
Singin' in the Rain 176
Singing Tall Tales (*Cantando mentiras*) 78
Sleep, Sleep, Baby (*Thula, thula, ngoana*) 113
Softly, Softly (*T'hola, t'hola*) 70
Soldier, Soldier 12
Somebody's Knockin' at Your Door 35
Somos el barco (We Are the Boat) 170
Son macarón 61
Sonando 20

Sourwood Mountain 44
Star-Spangled Banner, The 252
Starlight, Star Bright 182
Straighten Up and Fly Right 67
Streets of Laredo 134
Sweet Betsy from Pike 118

Tancovacka (Dancing) 114
Theme from New York, New York 119
This Pretty Planet 174
T'hola, t'hola (Softly, Softly) 70
Thula, thula, ngoana (Sleep, Sleep, Baby) 113
Tie Me Kangaroo Down, Sport 22
Tina singu 144
Tsuki (The Moon) 15
Turn the Beat Around 4
Turn the World Around 62
Twelve Days of Christmas, The 242

Wade in the Water 131
Waitin' for the Light to Shine 18
Walk in Jerusalem 58
We Are the Boat (*Somos el barco*) 170
We Go Together 26
We Shall Not Be Moved 249
We Shall Overcome 160
Weevily Wheat 57
Wheel of the Water, The 178
Wings of a Dove 154
Winter Fantasy 236

Xiao (Bamboo Flute) 152

Yibane amenu 153

NOTE: These page numbers refer to the actual page in this book. Page numbers for the Pupil Edition appear above the title of each arrangement.